HOW TO START A FARM IN 2020

THE STEP BY STEP GUIDE TO STARTING A PROFITABLE FARM IN 2020

ALEX JOHNSON

CONTENTS

INTRODUCTION

Farming is one of the most ancient professions in the world. It is the propeller for a civilized society, the foundation for all the food we eat and the products we use. Without farming, we would have nothing.

In today's world, farming can be a very lucrative business, but only if you are smart about it.

The point of this book is to talk about how you can make a farm profitable. You likely have some knowledge of the actual production side of a farm, but knowing how to turn it into a business where you make money is a completely different story.

As a business coach, I have helped numerous clients with their farming issues and have managed to coach them to success. Throughout this book, I want to go through some personal stories, practical examples, and insider tips on how to start your farm off in the best way possible.

It only takes a $1,000 yearly gross income from agriculture sales to be considered a small farmer in some areas. Even if it might seem impossible, I promise that by the end you will feel confident walking away knowing exactly what your next step is going to be.

HOW TO START YOUR FARM

⚜

*O*ne of the first clients I ever coached was actually a friend of mine.

He had a pretty good job, bringing in almost six figures a year with a decently high ranking at his job. He likely could move up, maybe in a couple of years if he continued to work as he had been. He had the perfect businessman lifestyle: a great apartment, a nice car, and could easily get a date with whomever he wanted. From an outsider's perspective, he seemed to really have it all.

He would go home at night, work out, and read up on business trends. He would go out to the hottest clubs and bars of the city on weekends. He had it all, and many of our mutual friends admired him. However, one day, when we were alone, he had a complete breakdown.

He lost it.

I had never seen a grown man cry so much. He revealed to me how miserable he was and that he was completely unhappy in his current position. Every day he would go to work with knots in his stomach, sick over having to carry on with such a boring career. He was completely dissatisfied, even though he was incredibly good at what he was doing. The lifestyle did not feel like it was his own, and he felt like he was trapped in somebody else's life. He said he didn't know what to do, and I was at a loss myself.

My expertise, up to that point, had been in coaching people for various businesses. I wasn't a therapist or a mental health counselor. I wanted to be a friend, but I didn't know where to start. Then he said one completely shocking thing, and it hit me. He was not the kind of guy that I ever would expect to hear this from. He told me, "I just want to move away, buy a farm, and start over."

I sat there in silence before I responded.

"Well, why don't you?"

He lifted his head up from his hands and looked at me through red eyes, almost like he had an epiphany.

Naturally, his immediate response was, "I can't. Of course, I can't, I have a job."

I asked him, "What is that job worth if you can't be happy in it?"

After a few more moments of silence, we started to really talk things out.

I reminded him of his strengths, like his ability to create a brand and market it towards the right people.

I reminded him that he was the one who helped himself to the position he was in now. Nobody else had handed him these opportunities, they were all things he had to work for. I talked about that time when he was in college and had to scrape pennies just to get by. He made it then, so he could make it now, if he had to.

The more we talked about it, the more he realized that he loved that part. It was the struggle and the fight and the push forward that kept him going. Once he had reached that peak point at his job (at least where he currently was), he felt like he was completely trapped. He could continue to work harder to get even higher, but it wasn't a subject he was passionate about. He came from a small town, and it turns out he missed that easy lifestyle, living in a nature-centered space.

He became the first farmer I coached.

Not only did I open the doors for him, but he did the same for me, and now we are both successful in our crafts. He had a bumpy road to start with, but he loved every minute of it.

The reason I'm starting off with this story is to

remind you that there is only one thing that is required from you for this to become your career.

Passion.

I am not an accountant. I am not a spiritual guide. I am not a financial analyst.

Maybe at times I have emulated the important qualities of these individuals, but at the end of the day, I am a business coach.

I know what it takes to really make it to the top. All of the little things you do financially to get you up there are different for every person. But one thing always remains true with every client I have.

Finding that drive and that passion inside of you is the key to starting your business. It doesn't matter what kind of experience you have, how much money you have to begin with, or where you currently stand in life. What is most important for finding success in a market such as this is making sure that you are passionate about it.

If there's one thing I want to reiterate and I want you to focus on as we travel throughout this book, it is finding that motivation, that spirit, that drive, and that will to succeed inside you and feeding off it to create the life you've always dreamed of.

Setting Business Goals

Before getting into the numbers and other financial aspects of business, one has to begin by understanding what their intention and purpose is for their farm.

You can't plan a wedding if you don't have someone to marry. You can't save for college if you don't know why you're going to college. You can't spend money if you don't know what you're spending it on!

To set a good business goal, the first thing you want is an understanding of what you want to get from this. That involves your purpose, your intention, and your ideologies. Are you hoping to contribute something good to society, or are you just doing this as a pastime?

Picking between this being your sole income and a hobby is also something you have to do for tax reasons. If you're planning to make less than $1,000, a year from farming, you are considered a hobby farmer. This means you won't need to abide by some of the same regulations or apply for the same exemptions that an individual who does this as their sole form of income will when filing taxes.

What kind of farm do you have? You can't just be a farmer and do it all. While it might seem like that is the case when we start singing children's Nursery Rhymes or watching people on movies, most of the time, farming is limited to a few operations.

For example, having cows, pigs, chickens, and crops is a lot of work. This is likely not something that you will be able to do on your own, unless you had one of each animal and your own small garden. When we talk about farming in larger terms, you want to pick your niche. You have to find a specific population to cater to, and most importantly, think about your intention.

Why are you farming?

Answer that question yourself right now. Why do you want to get into farming? Let's say that your response is that you're looking for a simpler life. You don't want to clock in at the nine to five every day. You want to be in charge of your own business. You want to take your finances into your own hands, and you want to restore your connection to nature. All of this is great and certainly something you can gain from starting your own farm. You should set as a first goal for yourself to start small, for example taking your products to a farmer's market.

Start by growing a variety of easy crops in your backyard and then take your harvest to the market. From there, once you discover what you truly like about farming, it's easier to come up with those goals and intentions. Some individuals have been farming their entire lives and their parents have taught them everything they know. For example, if you always wanted to be a dairy farmer because your parents were dairy farmers, you likely have a lot of knowledge. You can begin by focusing on that aspect. Just because you might not be sure about what you want to farm just yet, that does not mean you can't begin the process.

It all starts by planting that first seed. Get your hands dirty. Experiment with crops, and when you've managed that schedule, you can introduce smaller animals, such as chickens or goats.

Just because you're good at keeping houseplants alive doesn't mean you'll be good at having a farm. It's a much different category and it requires extensive work and knowledge. As soon as you put the pressure on yourself to make money from this, you also have to recognize the added intensity of your success. Farming can be a gamble for beginners who are not aware of their clear intention. You might run into things you did not even fathom. At the beginning, you could get a horrible fungal infestation of your crops, causing a nightmarish situation. You could have extremely sick animals that spread disease like wildfire among your livestock. You could even experience a devastating fire from not practicing correct protocols.

Farming is much more than digging a couple of holes and planting some seeds in the ground.

It requires hard work and you have to be ready

and willing to put that in. To set your goals, you first have to make sure they are realistic. If you've never been within a five-foot radius of a cow, you cannot realistically expect yourself to be a successful independent dairy farmer by the end of the year. Of course, if you can enlist the help of somebody who is an expert on the subject, that will dramatically increase your chances of success. Your goals should also be semi-specific. This first starts with what your intention is. Do you want to be able to be a full-time farmer by the end of the year? If so, you have to consider what your level of income would need to be.

Do you want farming to be a business that includes your family? Maybe you hope that you can have your children work on the farm one day. Having these bigger goals requires coming up with some more financial aspects. As a business coach, I normally work directly with my clients to come up with these goals. I don't know your specific situation, so I can't tell you how much money you'll have to make. This requires looking at your current finances now and deciding what the total income you will need to have as a farmer is. You also have to remember you won't be paying taxes in the same way. They won't get automatically taken out of paychecks. Instead, you'll have to pay quarterly taxes, and this can be a hefty sum in itself. You also have to consider the cost of monthly insurance covering all aspects of the farm, and the cost of the actual production, including any equipment, animals, seeds, pesticides, fertilizers, and so on. This all should be laid out in a comprehensive business plan.

When setting these goals, you also want to give yourself deadlines. As a farmer, it's going to be extremely important for you to have these deadlines in place. Much of the business you're conducting is going to be dependent on the seasons, so you can't overlook that important aspect.

Dreaming of being a farmer is incredible.

But a dream is not a goal.

The goals that you begin to set for yourself and your farm have to be specific and realistic. These are the most important aspects of any goal I encourage my clients to set.

Knowing Your Space

All of our land has a different kind of potential. What do you plan to use yours for?

When starting a farm, it's extremely important to know your space. A plot of land in California is going to have dramatically different results than one across the country in Ohio. Not only are the climates much different, but so are the rules and regulations that are in place in order for you to be a farmer. Before getting into this book, I think it's important that you become aware of any unique rules that might exist in your state to define what is legally allowed for your farm.

Zoning is a huge issue for many property owners. If your land is not zoned to farm, it is illegal for you to operate your business on your property without getting it rezoned. If you're just trying to plant your own personal garden, that's much different than conducting a lucrative business. It's also important to know your land and what the soil could potentially produce. If you live in a drier area, you're not going to be able to yield the same crops as someplace a little more humid. If you have luscious rich soil, that's great for some crops, but others might prefer sand or even clay. If you want to be a banana farmer, you're not going to be able to do that in the middle of icy Alaska. Your space will dictate much of what you can grow, so it's important to consider this factor as you are setting your business goals.

Understanding the Risks

The idea of farming is a desirable one by many. Having so much open space, the freedom to work as you need, and full control over your finances, all while working with nature is something to be desired, that's for certain.

However, there are a lot of risks that come along with it.

The first and biggest risk that many farmers face is the potential for financial downfall. This occurs if you are not properly managing everything necessary to conduct your business. You have to account for all costs and anything that you're going to be spending your money on. As a business coach, it's my job to make sure that you are looking at everything. I can't tell you what your dreams and passions are, but I can tell you what your state laws allow.

I wish I could be next to every single reader, coaching them through this process, but unfortunately that's impossible. I'm not going to be able to give you the specific zoning and legal restrictions in your area, and if I tried, you would likely get bored as I discuss areas that don't apply to you. However, what I can do is help lay out a solid foundation for you to launch your business from, as well as a visual checklist for you to follow throughout this process.

You should have a notebook next to you as you read, to take notes and make sure that you create a guideline for your own personal research. After we finish up the book, it's going to be up to you to dive further into those areas which apply to your situation. For example, if you're going to be a cattle farmer, you'll want to take note of the restrictions that are in place for farming livestock. You'll want to be aware of the different tools and steps necessary to create a humane and habitable place for your cattle to live. The biggest issue that my clients run into is that they underestimate the cost of starting a farm.

When you think of any business, of course, it sounds expensive.

You have to buy the storefront, you have to fill it with merchandise, you have to have all the proper permits and certifications in place, and so on. Starting a farm sounds so easy by comparison. You get to walk out your back door, and there is where your business can be conducted. However, farming crosses the line into food production, which has its own strict standards. Anytime you are creating something that could be consumed by the public, you have to be especially careful about the way that it is handled. Financial risks involve not considering the cost of obtaining certain licenses or creating healthy and safety protocols in place to protect you and your products. To avoid or minimize the risk of overspending, having a solid business plan in place is necessary. I will break down what should be in that business plan in a little bit.

You also want to look for ways to be frugal and

cut costs. This could be by buying secondhand items, or even renting certain equipment. It could include downsizing how much land you plan to farm from the beginning, and starting smaller instead. It might be even hiring extra help to increase productivity, or get a better expert look at how to grow your company.

Farmers also have to face many environmental risks. What if there's a flood? What if there's a drought? What if there's a tornado? What if there's a fire? Any of these things can absolutely destroy your business. The best risk protection for this is to have insurance in place for your farm. Insurance is yet another cost to consider for your company. If you are starting a farm that has many workers on it, you are also putting yourself at labor risks. If one of your employees gets injured while they're on the job, you are liable for that. You have to ensure their safety and protection, as they are handling treatment, handling chemicals and taking care of livestock.

There is always the risk that your product simply won't sell. You might be marketing to the wrong audience, or maybe competitors' prices are driving yours too low to have any profit leftover in the end. This is why a proper business plan, including a marketing strategy, will be essential. Finally, you have simple production risks such as not planting things correctly, or underproducing a crop, or simply the error of a beginner farmer. You have to account for all of these risks before investing everything you have.

Your Farming Mentor

One thing I want you to consider in this process is to have a farming mentor. This is somebody that you can look up to, who can offer expert advice throughout this journey. A farming mentor can be anybody from an old retired farmer to somebody younger who's simply been working on farms more than you. They don't have to be more financially or professionally advanced. The most important thing is that they have the knowledge and the firsthand experience to help work you through the kinks of farming. A mentor is somebody that you can hire and pay, or you can simply have them assist you in the process by offering different services in return.

A farming mentor might simply be somebody retired who's willing to help out the next generation. Whoever this individual is, have them go over your business plan with you. Discuss the weaknesses in anything that you might have forgotten. This is especially important for people who are farming in specific areas. They can help you become more aware of certain aspects or regulations that you might be overlooking. It is usually those weird rules or permits required that can get a new farmer caught up in bigger issues.

A farming mentor is also going to be there to encourage you and give you first-hand knowledge of mistakes that they went through themselves. They can let you know which setbacks you can recover from, or when you might have to completely try a new strategy.

Not all of us can find a farming mentor, but that doesn't mean the help isn't out there. Consider reaching out to online communities, and know that your community likely has farming assistant programs in place. This can be through your state or local government, or it could just be hobby groups within a certain area. The more sources and tools that you can pull in for your knowledge, the better you are setting up your farm for success. There are so many little things and issues you can run into along the way that as a new farmer, you can't afford to act as though you are immune to them.

This can be a risky and rocky business to start off with, so rather than waiting to make the mistakes yourself, give your mind the chance to be immersed in a totally new learning experience by learning from the mistakes of others.

Business Plan

Writing a business plan is important for farmers of all sizes. Even if you are using your own backyard to start the business you've dreamt of, having a solid plan gives you an idea of all the costs. The biggest issue my clients have is remembering to account for every last detail.

I'm not going to tell you how to make your business plan, but rather, I'm going to list the steps which need to be taken for a business plan. Not only does this give you a solid foundation to launch your company, but you might also need a business plan to help you take out a loan or find investors. It gives those who are considering giving you money confidence and reassurance that you actually know what you're doing.

The first part of your business plan is all about your personality. Make sure you consider:

- Background information
- Location
- Overall mission and message
- Goals for the future
- Goals for your finances

This can all be laid out accordingly in whatever order you think flows well with your company. Each should be a quarter to half a page of information. Go longer if you'd like, but this is more than just a brief sentence or two.

Consider if you're a family or a new business. Are you carrying on a legacy or starting your own? Where are you located, and how does that affect what your business is going to look like? An urban farm on a half-acre is much different than a farm in the middle of nowhere on 10 acres. Consider the climate and how this plays into what you're growing as well.

One thing I always coach my clients on is using a SWOT analysis. This goes for everything and can be used in all aspects of business. It involves your:

- Strengths
- Weaknesses
- Opportunities
- Threats

A quick example of a SWOT analysis I helped a client with in the past: they wanted to start an herb farm on the outskirts of a major midwestern city. Their strengths included the appeal, low competition (there weren't many urban farmers at the time), and the client had a long history of working on a farm as he grew up, meaning his knowledge was a valuable asset.

Then we went over their weaknesses. These included the fact that he didn't have much money to start up, and he was close to a low-income area that would likely be sticking to the larger and less expensive grocery stores. However, we also identified this as an opportunity as we went over different crop swapping events and community outreach programs as marketing tactics. Other opportunities were the various farmers markets that took place throughout the season, a different area every weekend. This allowed him to find the perfect market with returning customers who became life-long assets.

The threat was what any urban farmer had – a lack of space. If something bad happened to a section of crops. such as drought or infestation, he would be out for over a month until he could grow a new harvest. This was also the Midwest, meaning the seasons limited the crop time dramatically as well.

After you've done this part of your business plan, you can move onto the logistics and more financially structured aspects.

You would want to discuss the roles that various people would play. This would include:

- Management
- Team members such as harvesters, planters, etc.
- Investors

If you are a one-man team, lay this out in the plan too. How do you plan to operate this individually? If it's you and a spouse, what roles will each of you be playing? You would also need to have a breakdown of how many hours team members would need to work, and what rates you would be paying them.

Next, you would want to cover what your plan for marketing is. Where are you hoping to spread the word about your company? Lay out a budget that you would hope to be able to commit to for branding as well. Don't fear not having a marketing budget – I have worked with clients in the past who spent $0 on marketing in the first six months and still managed to grow. While you might not have to spend money, you will be making up for that in time. A lot of early growth comes from word of mouth and time spent on social media reaching out to customers. We'll talk more about organic marketing later in the book, but remember to mark this down as one area to give focus to when mapping out your company.

After your introduction, goals, employee break-down, and marketing plan are covered, the last two sections are your cost and profit analysis. This is basically the strongest foundation for your company. Having a great mission statement is meaningless if you don't have a solid plan of spending and making money.

When talking about a breakdown of cost/profit, remember it is all about:

- How much you already have
- How much you need
- How much you hope to gain

Let's think of this on an extremely simple level. Let's say you want to grow 50 pineapples. Right now, you have about $50 to invest. In order to get the right supplies, you need about $100. However, you're hoping to sell the pineapples for $4 each, meaning you'll be making about $200 after all is said and done. Where do you plan on getting that extra $50 to invest, and what would the interest be on that small loan?

Of course, when you're breaking down your budget, it's going to be in the thousands range, but on the simplest level possible, this is what will be included in a financial breakdown of your business plan.

To recap, remember that your business plan should include these important areas:

1. Introduction to who you are as a company
2. Goals and hopes for your business
3. Background information
4. SWOT analysis
5. Employee/labor breakdown
6. Marketing plan
7. Cost analysis
8. Profit analysis

At the end of your business plan, it always helps to ensure you go through anything you might have missed as an individual. Cover any unique circum-stances for your business, as well as touching briefly on bigger goals you hope to achieve further down the line.

There are countless business plan examples online that you can look at and compare your company to. Some are as short as 5 pages, others can go up to 50 or more. Start incredibly small, right this minute, with your business plan.

I want you to have a notebook or binder with you throughout this entire process. This is for you to take notes as we move along, and fill in all the necessary information. Think of it as a first step to the business plan. We've already touched on creating a mission statement, and you are the only one who knows the background info on your company. Before moving onto chapter two, take some time to go over this. It's ok to not have it all figured out right this second, and actually, you shouldn't try to. A lot of the important information will come to you as we keep going through the book, and new ideas will certainly be inspired within you as you dive deeper into the business side of your company.

I'm going to go over what your mistakes and threats might be, as well as how to recognize your strengths and opportunities. We will briefly discuss employees within this chapter, but that is something that doesn't apply to everyone, so I'm not going to dive too deeply into that either.

Marketing is another big area I will be going over, as well as tips and reminders on rules, regulations, and important accounting information. At the end of the day, I am a business coach above all else, and I want you to be as successful as you can with your company. I'll dive into soil science and caring for animals, but a lot of that information is something you likely already have an idea of. Most clients I've worked with have some background knowledge in farming as it is, so I'm not going to tell you how to farm, but how to start a farming business. Anyone could pick up a shovel and plant a seed, but it takes a dedicated, compassionate person to invest their time and money into this type of business. With the right tools, I fully believe you will be able to not only create a successful business, but to create a successful life.

Registering Your Business

Before you do anything at all, whether it's coming up with a name or planting that first seed, you have to do research on farming restrictions in your area. For U.S. readers, this can start by visiting the website of the United States Department of Agriculture.

On the highest level, they can help you come up with a business plan and even assist with finding financing.

Next, you have to decide what kind of business you are. This means choosing between:

- Sole proprietorship

- Partnership
- Limited liability company
- Corporation
- S corporation
- Non-profit
- Cooperative

This is very important because you can't change it depending on which you pick.

A sole proprietorship is when you are the sole owner and you accept all responsibilities, including losses or legal charges.

A partnership is similar, but these responsibilities are split between two people. In a sole proprietorship, depending on your business, you don't always have to register. For example, a single freelance video editor who works from home could be considered a sole proprietorship if they manage their own clients and aren't employed by just one company.

However, as a farmer, there will be a plethora of other regulations and rules you'll have to abide by, meaning it will be necessary for you to register your business.

A limited partnership is what you would be if you were doing all the work and had some investors who were behind the scenes. A corporation is a company with multiple shareholders who play an active role in major decisions. This is a company that has many employees and, well, a lot of money behind it.

You will likely then either register your small farm as either a sole proprietorship, partnership, or an LLC. An LLC is a medium between a sole proprietorship and a corporation. You can have more money from investors, while still not putting yourself at personal risk for losses.

About 4 out of 5 farms will be registered as sole proprietorships. The last one is a mix between the rest, with a majority being LLC.

What do I recommend you choose? For now, stay as a sole proprietor. This scares some because you will be legally liable for any losses. If your farm goes bankrupt, you're going bankrupt, not just the business.

However, once you start to establish your company more, work out branding, and resolve any other issues, you can then consider switching to an LLC. This is my recommendation, because it's not as easy to go from one to the next.

Take things slowly.

To actually register your business, there's no one single best way to do it, but multiple places you have to report to.

The first thing you'll do is register your business name. Be cautious of any trademarked names already out there. Check out the U.S. Patent and Trademark Office website, where you can search a ton of different names to see if yours is eligible for use.

The name should be something unique and specific to you. Take some time to choose the business name but remember it can also be your legal given or family name. For example, if your name is Alex Jones, your business name could be Alex Jones Farms. If you pick a name different from your own name, that can require a different certificate depending on your location, but it's usually a small fee less than $50; again, this is really dependent on your area. For example, in Illinois that fee is $5, but in Oregon, it can be as much as $50. In some states, you might also have to declare your business, which could include posting your name in a newspaper for several weeks at a time. All of this can be done at your local Secretary of State's office.

The next thing you will want to do is obtain your EIN. This is an employer identification number and exists for the government to be able to track your income and taxes. This is something you will be able to easily do through the IRS website. Please note that you do not have to have this if you're not hiring any employees, but it's still helpful for some financial purposes, such as taking out a business loan. You can also ensure it's easier to apply for worker's compensation, disability, and any other insurance that might be necessary if you have employees. To recap, the beginning of the registration involves:

1. Register your business name through your local Secretary of State's office
2. Obtain an EIN

After you've completed these basic steps, next comes ensuring you've obtained the right:

- Certificates
- Permits
- Licenses

This is what I'm going to go over in chapter two. Again, I'm only getting into these on the surface level, as there are so many restrictions and regulations that even if I were to only cover the 50 states in the U.S., it could be a whole series of books in itself!

Once you've acquired the right certificates, licenses, and permits, you'll want to ensure you have insurance coverage. This includes insurance for:

- Liability
- Workers compensation
- Commercial vehicle liability (if using automotive equipment)
- Equipment
- Homeowners
- Livestock
- Crop
- Continuation of income

On a personal level, life insurance will be important now more than ever for your farm because not only will people likely be depending on you, but you don't want to leave them with the massive costs of operating a farm if something were to happen to you.

Liability insurance helps, especially if you are going to have employees. As any property owner, this insurance will back you up in case of accidents. For example, let's say you live on a 10-acre farm. The neighborhood kids decided to play on part of your property, not realizing they couldn't. You weren't home at the time and one kid fell into a pit you'd dug and broke their arm. Of course, it's not a smart idea to leave holes unfilled, but accidents happen, and mistakes are made frequently. Liability insurance can help protect you in a situation like this.

Crop and livestock insurance helps to keep your money-making aspects in check. How can you make money if your crop has been destroyed? What do you do if all of your animals get sick and unexpectedly die? A continuation of income insurance also backs you up in case of natural disasters. Think about how a tornado or hurricane could completely wipe you out for over a year. Don't overlook the importance of insurance.

I'm going to get a little further into taxes and insurance in the final chapter, but for now, I want to simply reiterate that these are the important steps of registering your business:

1. Pick your name
2. Register your business name according to local guidelines
3. Obtain an EIN
4. Obtain legal documents (certificates, permits, and licenses)
5. Take out the right insurance

Necessary Tools

Some expenses are going to be costlier upfront, but could save you in the long run. For example, you could purchase a greens washer for farmers of lettuce, spinach, and herbs. It could cost as much as $500, but it could take what is normally a 5 hours job and make it into a 30 minute task, saving you costs on labor.

The tools needed are the most under-looked aspect of farming. I've had a lot of clients start with this business because they thought they could do it for $0 down. If you propagate certain fruits and veggies, you can grow them on your own without even needing starter seeds. If you already own a home with land, you can use that land to start your farm. However, with this mindset also comes the danger of overlooking many important areas of business.

You could potentially start a small farm for $0, but it's going to take years and years to see any significant progress.

Remember, your land isn't just going to be used for growing. You also need to consider the space needed for tools storage and cleaning and prepping your crops. It's best to purchase sheds or barns, or build them yourself, before laying out your business, so you'll know exactly what needs to go where. There's no point in having expensive equipment if you don't have a safe shelter to put it in. Tools can be expensive, even if it's just a hammer and a shovel. Keep your things secure in a locked barn or shed to ensure you won't have to use your equipment insurance.

Walk-in coolers are helpful for keeping produce fresh after harvesting. These are another expense that's costly upfront but could save you in the end. Letting your produce sit out in the heat as you farm could end up damaging it, or at least making it less desirable to customers.

Consider building things rather than buying them. As you're researching necessary tools for your farm, make a list of the equipment that you can easily afford, and what is out of your budget. From there, go on YouTube and Google and you will discover there are likely multiple tutorials that show you how to effectively build these things for yourself. Even if it's just a table to lay out your crops, you could save $100s by building it yourself. While it might be more labor upfront, it will pay for itself when you can spend that money elsewhere.

We won't get deep into every tool you will need but remember to consider the cost of crop and animal from the beginning to the end. This should all be laid out in your business plan. For every expense, consider:

- Price
- Quantity needed
- How long it will last
- Tax on the product
- Insurance needed

One of the biggest mistakes I see my clients making is that they only consider the price of one item. Farming is dirty work, which means you might be going through multiple things at a time. Protect yourself and your things by being as prepared as possible to pay for them.

Employees

You can't always do it all alone. A lot of my clients, farmers or not, have been wary of hiring help. The idea of someone else coming in and playing a role in your business isn't just risky, but also costly. However, it can save a ton of time, and even if this doesn't help you in any other area, it will at least alleviate some of the pressure and stress that farmers can constantly face.

The first thing you need to do is come up with your job descriptions. What do you want to hire people for? Are they going to be shoveling manure? Checking out customers at the farm stand? Operating a tractor? This is all-important because it will change how much you pay them and when and where they would work. Have the descriptions laid out to make the hiring process easier.

Come up with rules and regulations for your employees. Are you going to be doing drug testing? Is it required they have a certain degree or level of experience? Do they need to wear a uniform?

Next, you want to understand their pay. Will they be hourly or will they bill per project? Most farmers work hourly, though there are certain positions you could contract out individually.

Make sure you adhere to minimum wage standards and other safety regulations. This can mean posting signage and having certain protective pieces on various equipment they might be around. You might need to hire a third party to do payroll if you do not feel comfortable with the behind the scene taxation process as well.

A lot of farmers prefer to pay their employees "under the table." It's hard to track just how much revenue you might make when it's all cash, so it's easier at the end of the day to hand your employees a stack of cash than trying to go through the process of payroll.

I cannot urge you enough to NEVER do this. Paying them in cash is not illegal, but not reporting that is. If you are paying in cash, it's harder to keep a paper trail, which can put you at a bigger risk if something does happen, especially an audit of your company. When dealing with heavy machinery – and any business that operates mostly outside does – you are putting employees at greater risk of injury. Should you have to pay worker's compensation, you would need a solid record of their previous payments to keep a better record of things.

Financing Your Business

The more space you have, the more money you need. However, it's better to start with less money than more. If you have a small farm and $10,000 to spend, don't cap yourself out. Start with a quarter at a time. What can you buy with that $2,500? What is still out of this price range? Increase your budget slowly and only take what you need rather than taking all that you have. There are a lot of troubleshooting and unpleasant surprises in farming. While it seems easier than some other businesses, there is just as much room for loss as any other business. Not only is there the risk that your products (crops or animals) don't turn out as expected, but even once you have that under control, it's hard to make a profit from these things.

Some farmers I have worked with in the past prefer to only use their own money. The idea of taking out a loan is scary, what if you can't pay it back? The interest loans are also a turn-off. However, don't use all of your money. If you have $10,000 in the bank, you shouldn't expect that all to go to your farm. What if everything fails and you've drained your account? This is why taking out a small business loan can be very helpful. You can make larger payments with the money you do have, and you have the assurance that nothing bad happens. I had one client who refused to take out any loans. He hated being in debt and didn't' want to put himself at risk for being interest-gauged to the max.

He started his farm and the first year he did decently. He burned through most of his savings, so his profits weren't that great. The second year didn't do as well, and by the third, the weather was so bad it was hard to grow anything at all. He didn't just seek out taking out a loan at this point because he wanted to. Now it was because he didn't have any other option. Not only was it harder to find the amount he needed at this point with such a little income, but the interest rates were higher as well.

I don't advise everyone to take out the biggest loan possible. I simply want to remind you that to secure financing, you should start by making sure you have padding beneath what you're hoping to spend. If you have $10,000 in the bank but only think you need $7,000 to get started, that's fine. However, don't let yourself use every last penny of it or else you'll be in a much worse place than if you'd just taken out a loan to start with.

If you register through the USDA, you can set yourself up for success by working closely with experts to find a loan that helps you. There are specific agriculture programs that make funding more easily available to certain farmers.

RULES AND REGULATIONS A TO Z

⚜

I had a client once who had a medium sized farm. He mostly employed teenagers who needed extra cash over the summer to help him out. He was a very responsible individual and I helped him at a time when he needed to get out of a rut. He was struggling financially, and after working through some of the steps needed to boost marketing, we were able to provide him with a successful platform for creating a lucrative business. Before our time together was up, however, he panicked. He had just gotten a fine for improperly disposing of a chemical substance.

We sat together and tried to think of every possible thing that could have caused this fine to happen. He thought he had done his job. But it turns out something happened along the way that led to this issue.

After investigating this fine further, we discovered it was for paint cans. They were able to take the barcodes from paint cans found on the side of the road and trace them back to him. All of a sudden, I watched his face fill with rage. He had given two of the boys the task of throwing away the paint cans after they had finished painting the barn.

He wanted them to drive to the city's waste facility which was about 45 minutes away. This was on a Friday afternoon, so it's clear that the boys had other plans. Instead, they decided to dump the paint on the side of the road.

Not only did this make a mess, but it also leaked into some of the fields that were on the side of the road.

It was easy to spot the paint, after all, there was red splashed all over the pavement. Needless to say, these boys got a stern talking to, and my client laid out why this wasn't OK to do. They thought it was funny to see the paint cans explode on the pavement and figured it didn't matter as it'd get washed away in the rain.

They figured it was just like throwing a soda out the window, or any other kind of litter. That's bad in its own way. But it's especially harmful to throw toxic materials out the window.

It was on that day that I decided to take a deeper look into farming specific rules and regulations.

Of course, there are enough to create an entire

legal series on the subject, so I want to focus on widening your perspective and making you more aware of the areas in which you need to make sure you're protecting yourself.

When I work one on one with clients, we go through all of their practices to ensure that everything they're doing is legal and done in the right way.

However, the specific details are going to be left up to you, because I can't be there to witness everything you do within your business.

There are a lot of regulations in place. As a farmer, you are your most valuable asset, so it's important to protect yourself. Let's cover a few things that are absolutely illegal and should never be done within your business. Most of these are obvious, but there are still a few things to cover to ensure your safety is protected.

Agriculture Regulations

Before starting your business, you have to consider all of the rules and regulations that are in place.

The first thing that you have to do is consider what federal laws apply; these are things that cover every area in your country.

Beyond that, there will be state regulations that will also be important to understand.

The first category we're going to talk about is our agricultural regulations. These deal with anything related to the production and growing of your crops. As a business coach, I always have to remind my clients to consider all of these strict regulations in place. All regulations are in place in order to protect customers. If you are simply considering starting a farm to trade among friends, you might not be considered a business. Therefore, nobody is going to be protecting you. However, if you are selling to the general public, these regulations exist to ensure not only the safety of customers, but also your safety. By making sure that you have these protections in place, it's an acknowledgment that you're following necessary safety protocols with your consumers in mind. Anything dealing with food could lead directly back to you.

For the most part, many states do not require a business license in order to operate a small whole foods stand.

If you are only selling produce and nothing else, you likely can get away with simply selling at a farm stand. Again, every state is different and even counties within the same state can have rules contradicting each other.

I can't sit here and lay every single one of those rules out because that would take up three books or more worth of material.

One thing to remember is that as soon as you begin to sell market products that are broken down or mixed with other things, you are likely going to have to take out a business license. This would include making jams, pickled vegetables, salad dressings, or anything else you're creating in a way that alters the original produce. Mixing up ingredients and reselling them is considered producing a packaged product, and with that comes an entirely new set of regulations.

When it comes to farming crops, there are a few categories of certificates and permits that you need to consider. The first restriction is usually placed upon the type of pesticides you are allowed to use. Whether you can put these on your crops or treat your soil with them is dependent upon the product. What you have to keep in mind is if the pest control is labeled as having **restricted use**.

You might not necessarily have to get a certificate, but training is usually involved. Certification and training standards for any pesticides in your area can be further investigated on the **United States Environmental Protection Agency** website.

Especially when it comes to aquaculture, you will

want to refer to the **National Pollutant Discharge Elimination System** protocols. This carries into our waste chemicals section, but it's important to consider how this is going to be affecting your crops.

You won't necessarily be required to have a permit to get rid of certain pesticides off or on site. But you will have to adhere to important restrictions.

If you plan on doing any extreme types of forestry, this will usually require a permit. This would involve rock crushing, logs sorting, log storage, gravel washing, and the clearing of massive plots of land. Even if you own your land, you still have to be cautious about what you're doing on it.

When it comes to operating certain practices such as covered farm and uncovered farm, you're usually within your rights to do as you please when you have an annual income of $100,000 or less. The more money you make, the more careful you have to be because this means the further your distribution is.

How you grow your crops and what you do with them after in terms of storage isn't as monitored as the chemicals that you are using with them. Be extremely cautious about where you purchase your products and do your research on these individual chemicals, which will be treating foods that people are going to potentially eat. Remember to always be cautious about the runoff, and how it might affect the water in your area. There are also more regulations on urban farming and what you are allowed to do within a certain range of other people. Remember that your plot and the owned land you have needs to be zoned for farming as well. If you do something illegal and the authorities end up discovering that you're not even allowed to farm the land, that can get you into even more legal troubles.

Caring for Animals

Having animals brings on so many more regulations that you need to be aware of. The same goes for some of the chemicals, medicines, or any other treatments you might need to use on your animals. You have to be extremely cautious about how you throw things away. Don't ever assume you can just toss a can of medicine, cleaning supplies, or anything else like that in the trash can. While you might not think of this in your day to day life, there are many biohazards that you have to be careful of. Not only can they affect your farm, but they can affect the population around you as well. In terms of raising livestock, there are a few different sectors in which you will follow.

First let's discuss the selling of animals, whole, and not just for their meat. This would be done if you are a breeder who sells to other farmers. The sale of animals on your own property will usually fall within your own legal rights. Again, you really have to do your own research on the specific area that you are in. I could tell you that it's completely legal for you to sell a cow to another farmer on your property. But then I would just be talking about a state like Georgia. I can't say the same for all 50 states or countries outside of the U.S. as well.

When it comes to selling animals for their meat, this comes with a plethora of regulations. First and foremost, you have to consider the living conditions that these animals are in. They need to have the proper treatment and food/water standards met. You'll likely have inspectors come to your farm to ensure you are properly following these guidelines. The animals need to have adequate space as well. For example, one chicken needs to have four square feet of space. They need to have indoor and outdoor space, and the more you have, the more space you need to provide them with. Having four square feet for a chicken does not mean that you can have as many chickens as you can fit in those four square feet. In some cases, animal cruelty charges can have penalties bigger than just hefty fines, so these are extremely delicate regulations that you'll need to do extensive research on before purchasing animals to care for. When it comes to selling that meat and slaughtering the animals, this has its own set of rules as well. In most states, it is illegal for you to slaughter an animal on your property without proper licensing and certification.

Once you decide whether you are selling meat products or not, you will then have to determine where you plan to sell them. If you want to sell at a farmers market that is much different than selling to a commercial store. This requires different licenses.

These certification processes take months. That's why I'm not going to get into it now because this book is more focused on starting a farm, and you probably won't want to start off with slaughtering animals right away. It's an extremely expensive and extensive process and certification alone will take months at a time. You'll have to make sure that you pass proper inspections, and in some areas, inter-views or exams as well.

If you are farming a lot of animals, eventually, you might consider having a slaughterhouse on your property and that is its whole own enigma. Again, what I want you to really consider is starting your small business, rather than jumping into slaughtering animals and selling their meat, is to consider what you'll need to have in order to keep a *few* around. It's great for farmers to want to add on a few chickens to produce some eggs. But you have to remember that taking care of those chickens in a humane way is expensive and time consuming in its own way.

Waste and Chemicals

As a farmer, you will be liable for ensuring you're disposing of waste properly. It could affect the water system around you or at your farm if you're not careful. When we start talking about waste this refers first and foremost, to any water runoff. For example, if you have injection wells, you could be liable for tracking that runoff in an inventory, which must be submitted to the **underground injection control** in your area. Water runoff could mean the absorption of some of your harmful pesticides, and that needs to be monitored.

Hazardous waste is also something that needs to be monitored with extreme care. This includes any pesticides and chemicals to treat your garden. It could be motor oil and anything else to power your vehicles. It can be cleaning products, chemicals to treat water or a pool, and even paint. That's right!

If you get caught dumping paint on your property, that alone could mean some hefty fines for you.

Whenever you have excess waste you need to dispose of, it is best to check with your state and local governments to ensure you are doing so properly. Most areas will have a waste facility that you can safely and properly dispose of things in. Remember, it's better if you have to drive a little further to get rid of something safely, than to try to do it at home alone. Most of these processes will not require a certificate or license, but instead, simply a need for you to follow basic guidelines to avoid a fine. When it comes to using pesticides, as long as they are approved for regular use, you do not need a special certificate to use them. If you do discover if you're going to be using a massive amount of pesticides, and one that is **restricted for limited use** only, this will require a specific operating license.

Whether it is a restricted use or general use pesticide, you are not allowed to have an employee administer this on your farm without them having the proper license in most states. While it might seem tedious, you never know what dangers could occur, so it's best to be safe than sorry. This is one area that I urge my clients to study intensely when I'm working one on one with them. I will go over this individually and we will do investigative research ourselves. However, this book is going out to readers all across the world, so it's up to you to take that responsibility in your own hands. Everything should be easily located on the **Environ-**

mental Protection Agency website with links to resources, tools, and important reminders for all the rules you should be following.

When it comes to obtaining these different licenses and certifications, some of them will be costly. Some could be upwards of $300, and others might be as little as $25. The best thing to remember is the more you want to do, the more you're going to have to pay to do it. If you just want a small farm in your backyard to grow crops to take to your local farmers market as an independent worker, you're not going to have many restrictions in place. As we stated earlier, some states don't even require a business license to do this. However, if you're going to have acres of chemically treated crops and multiple animals, you're going to have to pay more for that. It will all be dependent on your geographical location and the intentions that you have for your business.

Your Land, Buildings, and Space

We all know it's important to manage waste and chemicals, and to treat our crops and animals in the best way possible, as they might be food for the public. One thing you can't forget about is the restrictions in place on your land. This includes your buildings, how you might use your space, and any buildings that you want to add to your land.

Any important building or construction is going to require a permit. This is a general approval that it is okay for you to do construction work on that land. If you're going into the backyard and building a few garden plots, it might not seem like you have to go and get a permit. However, some safety restrictions are in place for different reasons, and it's important that you check in with the relevant authorities before you undertake any work of this kind. For example, there could be an old well on your land that's been buried, and you don't know anything about it. By ensuring that you have the proper permits, somebody will be checking in and reporting on any potential danger that you might not know about.

Building small things on massive amounts of land that you personally own is a lot less regulated than building larger structures on a small land. The main thing to remember is how much construction disrupts the environment around you.

A small wooden box to plant herbs in your backyard is not very disruptive. A massive three-story barn next to your neighbors is.

Any demolition of old buildings also requires a

permit. This is especially true if you recently acquired an older farm and plan to bulldoze buildings. You never know what might have asbestos, for example. An inspector can help determine if you're at risk.

Painting could even require a permit, and this would be the case if you are going to be painting over or disturbing lead-based paint in any way.

These practices exist for a reason. Nobody randomly comes up with these rules and regulations just to torture farmers. It might feel like it sometimes, but there is always a reason, and usually it's for your protection.

It might feel like you could get away with certain things, like not buying a license or permit, but it will only come back to bite you in the end.

It might feel like you could get away with it because you've done it in the past. Just because you have a friend who's done so does not mean that the same laws apply to you. We all have a duty, and as farmers, especially, it's important that you go out of your way to protect the environment.

Not only could this destroy your business, but it could ruin your legal standing if you try to avoid the legal restrictions in place. Always double-check with state and local offices to ensure you're adhering to legal standards.

RAISING VARIOUS ANIMALS

I can't say for certain that this story is true because I only heard about it through barn chat as I was hanging out with one of my clients and his friends. He had a buddy over who told him a ridiculous story about a young entrepreneur who wanted to start a farm. This entrepreneur was always hopping to the next business venture. He had money to spend and he wasn't afraid to burn through the cash in his pockets. He had invested his own money earned from...his parents. As well as various trust funds from grandparents, of course. He was the typical guy with too much money and not a big enough brain to spend it the right way.

This entrepreneur decided that he was going to take over the dairy farm industry and become the top dairy guy in his state. He ordered one of the most expensive milking machines that you could get.

Everything was set up and he was excited for production on the farm to start.

Then he purchased the cattle, and they were delivered to his farm from across the country.

All of his employees immediately started to laugh, as the animals walked off the truck. He didn't know what was so funny.

It turns out he had placed an order for 100 bulls.

He saw that he could save money by choosing a specific vendor, and didn't realize there is a difference between a bull and a dairy cow.

When I hung out with this particular group of clients, they were often shooting the breeze telling funny stories. But regardless of whether or not this actually happened, it's pretty hysterical to think about. The most important lesson to take away from this is that money can buy a lot, but not always brains.

Before getting into more the business-related aspects of farming. I want to make sure that you are aware of the most common farm animals and the basic necessities they have.

Most readers know how to do this already, so we will talk on a basic and to-the-point level of what it means to own and profit from various farm animals. This is more of a guide on how to make the most of the animals rather than how to raise them. There are a lot of steps involving their health, vet care, and maintenance, all of which are crucial for the health of your livestock.

If you've never farmed in your life, consider hiring help to mentor you in the process. A chicken or two might seem like no big deal, but having horses and cattle is a very extensive process. Don't go into it blindly, because I've heard far too many horror stories of failing farmers that took on too much all at once.

You should also consider adding some of these animals to make your farm more diverse and add to income. If you have space that can't be used for crops, why not use it for a chicken pen? Even other small animals can be a profitable business, for example, if you consider raising rabbits for meat.

I'm going to give you a few tips to become more profitable with three basic categories:

- Poultry
- Goats and sheep
- Horses, cattle, and swine

All of these animals have different needs and potential to increase your farming income. Starting small with something like a few chickens, and working your way towards cattle or hogs is a great way to slowly step into the world of livestock. It's an entirely different life, but by diversifying what you farm, you're opening yourself up to more earning potential.

Poultry

Poultry is one of the easiest animals for you to raise, and it's my recommendation as the first animal for new farmers to start with. There are a few different types of poultry you can raise; the most common and the easiest is chicken, but don't forget pheasants, geese, turkeys, and fowls.

Most of these are great for their meat but you can also profit from selling their eggs. They can even help with some pest control as they like to eat and graze on little critters.

When considering owning chickens, you first need to decide what you want to raise them for. Are you raising them for slaughter, or are they simply to give you a few eggs?

To have a good sense of egg production, remember most hens can lay one egg, or even more in a day. You'll want to have both indoor and outdoor areas for them. Outdoor space needs to be at least four-square feet per chicken. This means if you have four chickens, you need 16 square feet for them to roam. They need space to stretch out even though they don't fly. They will also need a raised area for sleep, and to encourage the production of their eggs. When it comes to caring for them, they need constant clean water and food at the appropriate times throughout the day. You also have to consider regulations in place for selling their eggs. Even though you might be able to profit off of the eggs, there are different certifications and licenses to consider.

Chickens should have their own space and not necessarily be allowed to roam everywhere. They can be very destructive if they roam around your garden or plots, so give them their own pasture to roam in. What's most important for their protection is to ensure they are safe from predators. If you live out in the middle of nowhere, coyotes will hear your chickens and see them as a perfect midnight snack. Fences protecting them need to not only be tall enough, but also with small enough holes to ensure the chickens can't get out themselves. Chickens can be escape artists if you are not careful, and you would be surprised by their ability to fit through small holes. For all animals, and not just chickens, their water needs to be replenished multiple times a day and should be constantly clean. Feeding is dependent on the schedule that you will come up with for them, but water is something that needs to be there all day long.

Goats and Sheep

If you're not into poultry, or you don't want to put in that work, an even simpler animal to take care of is the goat. Some people, usually those who were raised taking care of cattle and pigs, think chickens are the hardest to keep of all animals. If you get used to raising certain animals, it can seem easy, but for beginners keeping smaller animals like chickens can be a good way to start dealing with livestock. Aside from that, goats and sheep, while bigger, don't necessarily require as much work, depending on their use.

You would be raising sheep for their wool, and both sheep and goats can be kept for their milk. Goat's milk is a very popular alternative to cow milk at the moment, and also offers a lot of beauty benefits. You'll frequently see it in soaps, lotions, and other luxury beauty and skincare products.

Slaughter animals and using them for their meat is its own entire enigma, which requires many more regulations and restrictions to be in place. You have to think about all of the antibiotics and medical treatments you'd be giving the animals, and how that;'s going to affect the meat, as it's going to be consumed by somebody. You can take your animals to slaughter at a slaughterhouse where they would be able to humanely kill your animals, and then process and package the meat for you. This is the best option for beginners, because slaughtering on your own land can be very tricky and there are a lot of things you have to remember. It's also very strenuous work and not easy for people to do, which is why I suggest avoiding slaughter unless you've been farming for several years already.

Sheep are very easy and go with the flow depending on the pasture that you give them might be. They are a lot less picky than goats about the type of grass they are on and enjoy eating weeds and foraging the land.

Many people actually like to have sheep and goats as an addition to their farm as they keep up with the weeds and act as a "natural lawnmower."

These animals are also great to have to prepare a pasture later on. For crop production, any animal can provide great fertilization to the soil. Consider crop rotation if, for example, you have two acres of land, you can use half for crops for one season, and then the other half for sheep. They can fertilize the soil and then you can go in and mix up the dirt for more productive crops.

For goats and sheep, an electric fence is fine as long as you use a smooth wire electric fence. Chickens only need four square feet, but a sheep needs 15 square feet per animal as a minimum, a goat needs around 10 square feet. Preferably 20 per animal is what you should go for if possible.

Sheep are a little harder to keep than goats because you have to ensure that you are shearing them on a regular basis, otherwise their fur can become very matted and painful. Both goats and sheep need to be protected and brought into closer quarters at night. They should always be in an enclosed space using pens with fencing to keep them protected when you are not monitoring them.

Putting bells on your sheep and goats helps ensure that you can keep track of them. If you do give them an outdoor space to roam at night, it's essential you have it within viewing distance so you can keep an eye on them. Many predators will go after them, so it doesn't hurt to have traps set up to protect your livestock. Make sure that you use humane traps that can help release animals to a different location once they have been trapped.

As I mentioned for chickens, you'll need to get on a schedule of feeding sheep and goats as recommended by your vet, in addition to making sure they have water, nonstop, all day long. This is especially true in hotter climates, where the animals are going to be outside with the sun blazing. For any animals you keep, you should have a vet come out on-site to ensure that you are looking after their health in the best possible way.

Horses, Cattle, and Swine

As I mentioned at the beginning of this chapter, this is just a quick overview of these animals. I'm talking about feeding, sheltering, and consideration of different costs and care that can make this process challenging.

Again, I'm no animal expert and I'm not a veterinarian. It would not only be unprofessional, but potentially dangerous for me to even give you specific feeding schedules for your animals. I can't act as though I am an expert on animal nutrition, so this is a specific area to be discussed with your veterinarian.

The point of this chapter is to make you more aware of the hidden costs and things you might not have considered around keeping livestock, especially with horses, cattle, and swine.

These are much larger animals that require a massive amount of space. I do not recommend anybody getting into this area of livestock business if they have never farmed in their life. Even if you've only farmed crops before, I still think it's important to be extremely knowledgeable before getting into the subject. While you might have been able to manage a 10-acre plot of land and all the crops on it, you aren't going to be able to have the same skills carry over into taking care of the animals.

For starters, pigs need their own personal pens and you should not have too many to one pen unsupervised. You can let your pigs roam during the day, but just like with any other animal, that space should be fenced, as the more free acreage to roam, the more potential to be attacked by predators. Pigs are very intelligent animals, and will often rub up against their cages if bored, or even start fights with other pigs. For this reason, it's important that you have a protective and strong metal fence when keeping them enclosed. Remember not to have an electric fence, as they will rub up against the side. An electric wire on the top of the fence can be okay, since they might not be running into it as often.

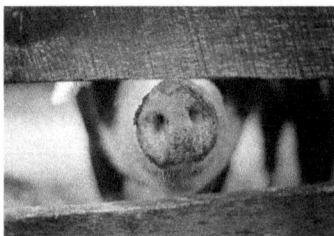

For cattle, you also need a considerable amount of space, and again for any farm animal, a constant supply of clean and fresh water is a must. The biggest expense for some of these larger animals is the food. This is one of the reasons I don't recommend getting into big livestock right away, because of the intense upfront costs. If this is an area you want to eventually expand in, you can build structures over time, and start creating their enclosures. Make sure that you have a barn and proper fencing. This alone can cost you thousands and thousands of dollars, so it can be something that you save and work towards as a goal for your farm. You also want to consider the sizable vet bills that can come from taking care of animals. If you have 10 pigs and just one of them gets sick, any illness can easily spread to the rest, resulting in massive veterinary charges. Animals like cows and pigs need inside enclosures as well as general shelter, such as trees. A cow might not want to go back inside the barn, so they'll stay outside even though they're scorching up under the sun. You have to provide them with shade through trees to ensure they do not harm themselves. Pigs could even get sunburned if their skin is exposed to bright sun rays for too long. You also have to bathe and groom the animals regularly. Pigs especially can have extremely dry skin, causing them to scratch themselves and rub up against fences even more.

You'll also need to weigh animals regularly to monitor their weight and ensure they are being properly fed. If you have pigs or cows, chances are you're using them for their meat, so proper weight management is essential to ensure that you're going to be getting your market value for them.

Horses and cows can also be very dangerous. Standing behind one can be enough to give you a concussion if they get spooked and kick you. Transporting them can also be dangerous. If you're riding a horse, it could throw you off, or if you're walking a cow, it could jolt away, causing the rope to damage your skin or even breaking your hand or arm.

Your animals will also need to be cleaned often. If you have pigs, you have to clean their pens. Contrary to popular belief, pigs are not dirty animals and require a clean environment. Maggots can easily fester in their feces, and if you're not cleaning the pens up regularly, you can have an infestation problem on your hands pretty quickly. Flies can cause bites and sores on the animals, which could lead to infections. You want to provide all your animals with fresh hay to lie on, and clean and bathe them regularly to prevent any infections.

You'll have to make sure that your barn has vital things like a fan to help keep the animal cooled down during extremely hot summers and a heater depending on the climate you're in, and what animals you have. If you're breeding animals and you have babies in the late summer, it's important that they have some sort of heating source during the upcoming 10-degree winter.

I've never coached somebody to start a massive

livestock business right off the bat; anybody that has gone into the cow or horse industry already had previous livestock knowledge. If you want to start a new adventure, that is perfectly fine, but keep it small. Even having one horse can be a massive expense that could put you into debt if you're not properly managing your finances. A horse can help carry you through your land and can even be used for old fashioned machinery. But remember, it's also a cost in itself, so sometimes it can be more cost-efficient to rent or loan your equipment.

Animals also carry their own financial risks as well, such as potentially losing them all to disease or a terrible accident, which is why insurance is also important to cover these losses.

Soil for Animals

Remember, having the right soil isn't just for crops. You also have to create the optimal soil conditions for livestock.

The soil your animals live on determines their comfort and what they eat. Your soil should be its own ecosystem with aggregation and hydration to keep it thriving. It should be a biological network that contributes to the continual enhancement of your farming conditions.

Pick where you plan to have livestock and take the necessary steps to create a healthy ground. There is a certain cycle to follow to get the best results. If you're purchasing livestock, this will likely happen between the spring and summer, so you need to begin to prepare your pasture in the fall by stirring and overturning your soil for growth before the ground becomes frozen. You'll plant the seeds before the winter for growth in the early spring.

As the grass begins to grow, create a rotational system of where you'll plant for the best grazing for cattle or other livestock.

Plants are an entirely different topic, and what most small farm starters are going to be concerned with. To help your business control costs, maximize growing potential, and make the most of their by-products, I've created a guided chapter on soil science for starting farmers.

SOIL SCIENCE

❦

*A*big area of focus that I go into every single situation with a new client is looking at every way that we can cut costs. Too often, people start with obvious things to cut. They think about necessities versus wants, and often have to make sacrifices that leave them unmotivated and disappointed.

It's great to be frugal, but if all you ever spend your money on are necessities, it can be hard to truly thrive. You could be spending money on new equipment, but instead, you have to spend it on something like soil or feed, it can be very taxing on your budget. I had a client who desperately needed to rework her pasture. She wanted to bring in pounds and pounds of soil, fertilizer, manure and anything else needed to make this the optimal place to grow. The cost of doing all this was in the thousands. It was one of her biggest expenses, but the land she had at the time was not doing her any favors. She did have a few small plots that she could play around with for smaller crops, but she still had acres that she wanted to make over. She was considering taking out a small business loan that would take her years to pay back. Instead of doing this, I asked if it would be possible for her to wait for a year and focus on something else instead. She looked at me annoyed at first. Why would she wait so long? I explained to her that instead of investing her money into all these crops, she could use it to buy some goats and sheep. They would be able to adapt to the pasture easily, and could help resurface the land. She could plant grass seeds to add moisture back into it without having to do too much tilling. She could also use the natural fertilizer she had available from the livestock manure, while also working on building up a strong compost. Over time, she could sell the milk from the goats and sheep, while also having a small garden of various simple plants on the parts of the land that seemed fine to use. She wasn't too excited about being patient at first, but she was excited when I was able to switch around her budget and make it more efficient. She ended up having a thriving pasture within about a year and a half, while also building a business solely around goat's milk. She got rid of the sheep because they became too hard for her to care for, but she ended up spending more on adding goats to her farm. She was able to plant a huge pasture, almost doubling her yearly profit. It took some convincing at first, but ultimately she ended up making the right decision. When cutting costs is hard, sometimes you have to figure out how you can work with what you have. Soil is incredible in that way. It can be very adaptable to whatever situation you might have, providing you with greater opportunities on your farm.

MOST PROFITABLE CROPS

When starting your farm, obviously you want to pick the crops that are the most profitable. However, sometimes finding a unique crop can be a better bet, depending on availability in your area. We will go over that later; for now, we are going to cover simple, common, and popular crops for you to consider growing. This means you'll be able to make the most out of your available space.

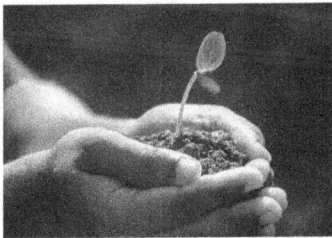

Picking crops that you are passionate about is also important. However, don't pick things that are very niche or very difficult to grow. For example, trying to start a pineapple farm in the middle of Indiana is likely not a profitable investment. If you're passionate about pineapples and you really want to do that, by all means, nobody is going to stop you. However, if you hired me as your business coach in order to help you make money, I would first encourage you to begin with the things that are the most profitable. One great place to start is simply planting a selection of leafy greens like kale, spinach, arugula, and lettuce varieties. Not only are these plants extremely easy to grow, they're also always in high demand. Every household would likely have leafy greens of some kind in their fridge at all times. Not everybody is going to consistently buy dragon fruit, mangos or pineapples. Vegetables like spinach and arugula are found in many dishes, so they are very popular for weekly groceries. They can rot easily if you don't properly care for them at home, so people might be purchasing these things multiple times a week. They pretty much grow themselves and require very little from you, so it's a great way to get started when beginning to understand how crops work.

Another great place to start is with soybeans and legumes. For people who have never farmed in their life, I would recommend starting with one of these.

These plants help cultivate the ground in their own way, meaning that the next crop you choose to grow can thrive even more because the soybeans or legumes have already laid out a pretty solid foundation through oxidation.

Tomatoes are another extremely easy crop to take care of. If you were to abandon your tomatoes for weeks at a time, they may potentially continue to grow because they are so resilient.

It's important to know that when it comes to produce like tomatoes, berries, apples, cherries and other vegetables and fruits like that, it's going to take a while to get them to a point where they are edible. For example, your first cherry tree season might have very tiny and very sour cherries. Your first round of tomatoes might produce only tiny, bitter tomatoes. These plants can take a while to really grow, so be patient. That's why it's good to have two or three crops to start within a small setting, so you can alternate between what you are producing.

Herbs are a very profitable and easy way to start a farm as well. Include basic things like basil and cilantro in your crop, but don't overlook more desirable herbs like parsley, rosemary, chives, saffron and others like that. Try to avoid produce that's extremely cheap at the store, for example garlic or even onions.

While garlic is good pretty much all year round, it's very cheap and you can likely buy a ton of it for less than or around $1/$2. You could still grow it and make a profit, but it might not be as popular in the farmers markets. Consider seasonal and delectable food that is more than just a staple. For example, peaches can be purchased at most grocery stores all year round, but they're really good in the summer. The same goes for plums and cherries.

By picking these seasonal fruits, you'll get people excited about your produce. When they walk by a stand and see bright yellow juicy peaches, they're going to reach for those first instead of the more easily accessible produce. Remember, farming is not just about edible things either. There is actually a great way for you to ensure you can avoid some of the more expensive certificates or other registrations necessary for growing edible crops. Flowers are always popular. People love to buy bouquets to take home to those they love, or they just simply enjoy having flowers around the house. Consider growing multiple types of flowers to create beautiful arrangements. Another example: lavender is a very in-demand herb and flower which is used in many different ways. If you pick aromatic flowers such as lavender, or a popular flower like roses, you can ensure that people are going to want to buy your product.

You will get to know what you're good at taking care of and what does well depending on your area after trying out a few things. Once you invest in all of the necessary equipment, such as cleaning machines and harvesting equipment, you'll have it to use for your next crop. You don't always have to be afraid of spending your money on seeds to start as long as you're giving yourself the proper time to have a trial period. If you're expecting to have a profit by the end of the year, of course it's not going to be as easy to experiment. But if you give yourself that room to experiment and even fail, it gives you a better chance to really know your market. Of course, the most important thing to remember about producing these profitable crops is to pick the optimal soil.

Types of Soil

Soil seems like just dirt. It's just dust on the ground. It's mud. It's a bug. It's old rocks and it just seems so meaningless.

If you really want to insult somebody, tell them that they're older than dirt. You would tell them they're dirty. You would complain if something was covered in dirt.

We say we treat things, well... like dirt when we don't care for them, because we don't think dirt is that important.

However, dirt is life. It provides us with so much necessary to thrive.

At this point, I hope that you have had at least a house plant in your life. While farming is not indoor gardening, if you're planning to start a farm, the care of a living thing is important to consider if you hope to be a successful planter soon. I want you to think about a houseplant you've had now. There has probably been a time where you moved it from one container to the next. When you did this, you got a chance to see all the plant's roots. What happened as it grew in that container is that the dirt was converted into more plants!

The thing about dirt is that it provides food to plants. If you were to plant a seed in a small container, that seed would grow, and eventually the roots would take over the dirt no matter what the type of plant is. Once you pull that plant out, there isn't as much dirt there. The plant was using that to grow. Where did you think all of that energy came from to help turn your little plant into a big one? While a lot of it comes from sun and water, plants also get essential minerals and nutrients from the soil beneath them.

The first and most common type of soil for

farmers is loam. Loam is what you would be using for any root vegetables and any leafy greens, tomatoes, carrots, and potatoes. This kind of produce does well in loam because the blend between dirt and sand helps give optimal drainage to make sure these root veggies are getting everything they need underneath the surface.

Another type of soil is peat. Peat is a little drier and more well-drained, and often mixed with compost. Peat is perfect for people who want to use their own compost from food scraps. Be wary of compost with high acidity, such as from any citrus fruits you've composted. Acidity is good in peat, but too much can kill off your plants.

Silt is another type of soil that offers similar benefits and would be used for drier climate fruits and veggies. Citrus trees, pomegranate trees, raspberries, blackberries, beets, and cabbage, all do very well in either silt or chalk. Silt is also commonly used for growing artichokes, cabbage, and even rice.

Sand is another important soil to consider. This would be best for anything that grows beneath the surface, or in drier climates. This includes pomegranate or fig trees, as well as herbs like thyme and juniper. Carrots, parsnips, and other root veggies also do well in sand, but remember they still need hydration just as if they were using loam.

Clay is not recommended for anything that grows beneath the surface, such as root vegetables, because it is so dense. Clay is better suited for planting long-lasting trees, for example cherry or maple trees. The same goes for pear or walnut trees: they work well with the clay and the density that is involved, along with the right humidity and pH levels, all of which are balanced naturally within this soil.

You're pretty much limited to the soil that you already have in the space naturally, but you can enhance it to accommodate whatever crops you're growing. For example, if you are in an area with all clay, you're going to be stuck using clay. That's when you would pick the most profitable produce to be grown within clay.

If you have regular loam, you can use fertilizer to help replenish this soil; it's beneficial to have alternating crops because the rotation will balance the pH of your soils. Plants like legumes or sunflowers are great at replenishing the oxygen within the soil, which will help your next crops thrive. You should also have animals roaming your pastures when you're not planting, as their feces will help naturally add fertilizer to your land.

Of course you'll be doing some tilling and other important preparations, so you don't have to think about it as if you're using excrements to fuel your food. It all gets mixed naturally together, and constant hydration from the rain and other natural resources help create a thriving ecosystem for your crops to grow.

Optimal Conditions

There are a few optimal conditions to consider when you are creating a healthy farm for yourself. The first thing to remember is that just because your soil is healthy, it does not always mean that it is going to produce the best crops possible. Healthy soil is important because that means it has proper hydration and dehydration necessary in order to sustain the correct level of water.

However, that does not mean that it is optimal for growth for all crops. Healthy soil could be enough to maintain that right level of nutrition needed for crops next year. You could use it as a pasture in the meantime, and allow fertilization to happen naturally from the animals grazing on it. In order to test your soil, it's important to take samples all throughout the year, rather than just bulk testing all at one time. The next thing you have to consider is what you're trying to grow. Some produce, for example root vegetables, like more of a dense environment, because it makes trapping the water easier. Sometimes, water can sit at the surface and doesn't go down to where the roots of the plant truly need it.

You might need to include tillage practices in your soil to get it mixed up. If you are planting something like leafy greens, it's better to make sure that area has a rich and blended soil, rather than something dense that you might use for potatoes and carrots. The prime conditions of your soil are dependent on what the prime conditions of your farm would look like. How big are your crops, and what are you hoping to yield through that production?

Remember that you should be using your soil for many different uses. You won't want to grow cabbage year after year. You need to alternate between different vegetables to give something back to that soil. Don't forget that an irrigation system is also necessary if you don't think your soil is going to be getting the right amount of drainage.

This includes having underlying pipes beneath where you are planting it to allow for that drainage. If you have a larger land, it's important that your crops are elevated, and you have trenches for dealing with rainwater. Like I mentioned earlier in the book, too much water runoff from your land could potentially cause damage elsewhere, so you should be following safety protocols and ensuring you have any and all permits necessary for planting or trench digging.

The process of fertilization is absolutely vital. You want to give something nutritious back to your soil, rather than having it just be dust and sand. You can use your own fertilizer through composting or animal waste, but it is also something that you can easily purchase. Remember that soil isn't just something on the ground; it's going to be an extra added cost in itself. You have to think about fertilization, the labor and time it takes for tillage, and necessary measures to ensure it remains properly hydrated. If you drown your plants in very deep pockets of water, you are not encouraging the healthiest growth possible. The same goes for under-watering them. While it's a much more involved process than just having an indoor garden, the same principles apply. The effects of over and under watering can look very similar on plants, so really get to know your crops to make it easier to troubleshoot the issues.

Troubleshooting Issues

Any issue with hydration can result in a big issue with crop production. If you're not properly managing the hydration of your crops, it can result in huge and expensive issues.

Hydration practices in farming might be one of the most challenging things you're going to have to deal with. To troubleshoot these issues and really determine what it is that you can do to get better results, it's going to take some trial and error.

One important thing to make sure that you do all the time is to cover crops. These are things like seeds, grains and even simply grass that you plant in between your harvests. This happens post-harvest and pre-planting, to help ensure that the hydration remains in that soil.

You also want to consider any leveling that's necessary to overcome issues with proper drainage and hydration. Leveling is necessary if you notice that part of your crops are doing well, while others are not. It could be that they are not getting the right amount of sunlight, either. If you're farming, chances are you have an open area where the sun is plentiful, but consider any trees that may be blocking certain sections of your garden, if you are planting your crops in a more foliage-crowded area.

Don't get too tillage-happy right away, either. Sometimes farmers think they need to constantly be mixing up their soil, but there are some circumstances where it's better to let that water sit. If you are not planting anything, sometimes the water is best trapped underneath the surface of the soil, rather than spread throughout. This is especially important if you believe or know that you're going to be going through a drought.

Let's say that you are still in the middle of the summer, before trying to plant an autumn harvest. If it's been particularly dry, you should assume it's going to stay that way. Instead of tilling, you might want to plant as the water beneath the surface will be able to spread back out to the roots in a more natural process.

This is something you will need to experiment with, so be cautious as you could just as easily drown a plant when you're really trying to water it.

HOW TO MARKET YOUR FARM

One client I helped coach had a failing business. He had inherited the company from his grandparents and it had been passed down from generations. He planned to pass it on to his children one day as well. Upon looking at the business model, it was pretty standard, except there wasn't any sort of marketing.

He was great at being efficient with costs and cutting down on labor or any other expenses. But it still wasn't enough.

The biggest issue for the lack of income was that he had no exposure. He wasn't creating a brand or marketing his business towards any one customer in particular. He was a very stoic man with little words to say, it was hard for me to get a sense of his personality out of him.

So I asked instead if he had any pictures of the

farm. I asked if he had a little background information so that I could start to do my own research.

In all solid family farms, there's always a story waiting to be told. Boy, was I right.

As he pulled out a huge plastic bin filled with memories, I was thrilled. Inside were pictures of weddings that had taken place on the farm, and even a picture of one of his relatives holding a newborn baby they had just delivered in the bedroom.

There were animals from decades ago, and crazy farm equipment that you can't even find in some museums. I was floored. This was exactly what his company needed.

He was very interested in selling pickles, and he had a great recipe for a popular barbecue sauce. Friends and family loved his cuisine, but he just wasn't marketing it right. The first thing I did was enlist in a freelance logo creator and font designer. We came up with the perfect aesthetic to match the photos that he had shown me. We then used clippings of his grandparents and of some of the beautiful events that had taken place on the land in order to help market his brand. Within a year, he was making it into small stores around him with his barbecue sauce and pickles on the shelf. He truly had a mom and pop style farm that had been handed to him, but he just didn't know how to market it right. It's that exact kind of personal connection and touching story that can truly help your business thrive. Customers are desperate for a personality in the products they buy, now more than ever, so it's important to remember to use tools such as past memories. They can help tell the story of you and your family as well as your business, making it more popular and recognized in your area.

Branding Your Farm

Now we are transitioning away from the more practical side of starting your farm and instead it's time to focus on branding. What does it mean to brand?

Well, this is going to be one of the most important things that you are going to do for your farming business. A brand is all about your image. It's about who you are and the products that you're trying to sell. A strong brand is one that knows itself. It's a company that has a vision and an idea.

The first thing that you'll need for your brand is a mission statement. What are you hoping to do? Think about the most successful company you can at the moment. It's likely to be a tech company, or a business that provides electronic equipment to millions of people all across the world. The mission statement for them might be that they want to provide excellent service.

They want to increase accessibility and relationships between people. These brands have a vision that they hope to achieve from a long standpoint. What is the mission statement for your farm? Do you hope to provide food to different people? Are you hoping to improve and protect the environment? Are you looking for nutritious ways to enhance people's lives? Whatever your mission statement is, that is completely fine. The most important thing is that you have one, and that you know what it means to cultivate this kind of brand.

After that's settled, you need to focus on your aesthetic. This is about the feelings you want to evoke, the tone you want to associate with your farm, and what emotions you are providing to your customer base. Many farms will be branded in a pretty rustic way. They'll use aesthetics that bring to mind wholesomeness ideals surrounding family, and values that are rooted in traditional life. This is perfectly fine if you want to go that route, but remember, you don't have to follow blindly.

Lately, many farm brands are choosing a more minimalist approach and a modern aesthetic. They're picking calm-inducing, clear colors and connecting back to nature, rather than focusing on the farm aspect alone.

Once you come up with your look, feel, tone, and aesthetic, then you have to pick a logo. This is going to be on your products, if you are crafting any. For example, if you hope to make candles, lotions, oils, dressings, sauces, or anything else that is going to be sold in a package, you're going to be putting your label on it. You're going to have your logo, your name, and any other information that customers need to get a better sense of who you are on your label. All of this is important for brand creation, because it's how you expand your company. If you are sending people home with products with your logo on it, their friends and family are going to see those. They're going to ask them where they got your products: that is the root of organic marketing.

Your brand is also going to appear on your social media, your website, and any marketing material you have. It can be on the sign that you have at the farmers market or the logo on your van as you deliver groceries to people around your town. This is important because it's what helps you establish yourself as a company. People want to go back to brands they trust. They're going to choose you because you provided them with exactly what they were looking for. By giving them a logo, you're giving them a signal and a sign that makes it easier to recognize who you truly are. Your brand logo and marketing materials may seem like just fun, colorful stuff, but they are absolutely essential tools for creating a lucrative thriving business.

Your brand also needs to be understanding and inclusive of the audience that you're targeting as a farm. For example, you may want to be focused on families and older individuals with basic nutritional needs, or on hip people passionate about cooking with fresh ingredients.

If you're branding a vampire romance book, your target audience would be teens. If you're branding heart monitors, your target audience is the elderly. If you are creating mustache wax, your brand is going to be male adults with facial hair. If you are creating baby blankets, your brand is going to be new parents.

Who is *your* target audience?

It's important to get to know who your target audience is, so you can shape your brand to cater to them. This is why, if you are starting a farm, you're likely going to pick those wholesome family feeling-inducing imagery, because that is the type of customer who is going to be purchasing your product. Of course, you could take an edgier route and do something grungier that would be similar to a metal band's aesthetic, but you would have to consider if this is going to attract the audience that you want. You might find a specific niche of metal-head farmers, but that's not as big of a market as staying general and catering towards families. By branding your farm in a certain way, you're getting a better sense of who you are and what you are trying to do. This will reflect in your core values, so as you navigate this crazy world and are confronted with more business opportunities, you can always go back to your vision to make sure you are still aligned with that mission statement.

Creating a Target Audience

Creating a target audience is going to be your way to ensure that they keep coming back. Reaching out to people and getting those first-time customers is incredibly important. That's how you grow your audience. However, if everybody comes at once and then they don't come back, that's not a sustainable business. You might have done great with your numbers in the beginning, but now you're falling flat because people aren't coming back.

You have to create a relationship with your target audience in order to really propel your brand towards success.

The first thing to do to recognize your audience is to understand the need that you are fulfilling. Now if you are selling, for example, lavender, you're going to be marketing towards people who use lavender for different reasons, whether it's to add scents for their candle company, as an addition to creams or lotions, or just to have in the house as decorative flowers. That is a much more specific audience than if you're growing spinach, tomatoes, or carrots for people to buy and eat.

What are you providing to people? What problem do they have that you've managed to solve? These are the questions you need to answer in order to understand who your audience is.

You also want to consider the spending habits and the budget of your audience.

If you are going to be selling in your front yard from a farm stand in your local community, people are probably looking for accessibility and low prices. They want to go to you, not just because they appreciate your business, but because it's easy for them. They'd rather stop at the farm stand across the street than drive into town just to grab a few tomatoes. If you are taking your products to a farmers market where there's a lot more competition for high-quality organic foods, that is going to give you a different customer base, and potentially different profits. Remember, your target audience doesn't have to be direct to the customer. You also have to consider stocking grocery stores and other local markets in your area. How can you brand yourself for that?

You might not be going for that wholesome family corner stop farm stand aesthetic. You could simply be going for massive productivity and high-quality products. That is a great way to get you into the homes of many Americans, either directly through end-consumer purchases, or through their favorite grocery store first.

You want to give an audience a sense of your personality. You have to share something with them that nobody else does. Not only are they choosing you, but they're choosing you over other people to go to buy vegetables in the first place.

You have to provide them with a reason to pick you every time. It could be a small incentive, such as giving them a free produce item with a certain number of purchases. It might be something bigger, like a 10% membership discount. You could also be simply cheaper than anybody else in your area, or you might have the best produce. Maybe your produce is the most aesthetically pleasing, and the taste is something to die for. Whatever your niche is, you have to find it and refine it. Articulate that point and let that be your driving factor.

Whatever your strengths are, they will propel you towards success and expose your weaknesses along the way, enabling you to better overcome those as well.

Social Media and Outreach

Once you've figured out your audience and your brand, it is time to get the word out there about your farm. This is done first and foremost in your local community. It's simply having a sign in your front yard to let people know that you are selling produce. You'll want to hand out flyers at different events, and see if you can post advertisements in different stores. All these good old-fashioned marketing tactics can still help you get the word out. Beyond this, it's time to get online. This includes social media, where you can better reach out to those target audiences.

Sometimes you're going to have to reach out in ways that don't provide you with instant returns on investment. For example, you might reach out to resources in the community to help spread your brand. This could be done by donating food to a local school. You might provide supplies necessary for different programs as well. You could even have students or community groups use your farm to learn. If you have acres of land you could potentially gift a portion of it to a local youth after-school group that focuses on growing crops to keep kids out of crime. It sounds extremely specific, but it does exist. That farm life could help them better connect back to their community.

The next step for you to take is to get into farmers markets.

People are looking for cheap, healthy, and organic options. People don't want to go to big box stores to get bruised, packaged produce anymore. They're looking for wholesome ways to connect back to their community and reach out to others. While it might cost more than what you could potentially make in a day at a farmers market, getting a booth is worth it. Don't stick to just one area either. If you live in a larger city and are an urban farmer, there are going to be many more opportunities for you to find farmers market areas. Even if you have to drive an hour a few times a week, going the distance can provide you with more income later on. Once you have started that outreach to customers further away from you, you can then focus on continuing to bring people back through your brand online. Any one of these steps can be challenging, so don't be afraid to reach out for additional help.

There are people who can strategically market your product in the right places. There are brand specialists, people who have gone to college to study these specific tactics, who can be hired to help. The same goes for when it comes time for you to take your brand online. It can be a very scary and challenging world to navigate once you put your brand on the internet, but in today's society, it can be one of the most profitable ways to ensure your business thrives.

Your Website

The first purpose of a website is to spread brand awareness. If somebody sees your logo, they can look you up online. Your company should be easy to find online and the website needs to provide more information on your brand.

You want your customers first to be greeted with your branding. They should easily see a logo, and even a mission statement can help. You want to use colorful images and design to keep them scrolling through the page. You have a split second to get people attracted to your brand, so if you're not putting all of that effort into that initial click they give to your page, you could be losing out on a lot of customers.

It's important to remember the limited opportunities we have to gain attention from these followers, and the impact that can have on our profits. You can give useful information to generate repeat visits, for example provide hours of operation, and locations of different farmers markets you will be at on a dedicated page on your website.

Your website also exists to help provide your customers or potential customers with a way to reach out to you. If a larger store stumbles upon your product, they might want to carry it on their shelves. They could really like what you stand for and see that you are doing well at a local farmers market, deciding to reach out and create that relationship. You want contact information to be available, whether it's a phone number or an email address, so customers can get to know you. Aside from providing general information, your website should also have links to your social media. This way you can grow your potential to gain that following on different platforms like Facebook or Instagram.

Your website can also be where you conduct sales, or have people place orders. By allowing people to place online orders, it's easier to know what you have to work with. You can prepare things for different customers and come up with ways to ensure that everybody is getting exactly what they want. You could potentially cut out having to go to the farmers market altogether and instead only focus on fulfilling online orders.

While farming seems like a very nature-centered outdoor activity, a lot of the branding you do is going to occur online now more than ever before. One of the biggest aspects of maintaining an online presence is learning to use your social media.

Social Media

Social Media is free, at least most platforms, and it is one of the best ways for you to have organic marketing for your brand. You should be on Instagram and Facebook at the very least, but Twitter and LinkedIn are also profitable websites to post on for businesses.

Even creating a YouTube account is a great way to garner more attention to your company.

Sometimes reaching out on social media, means that you have a following across the country and while they might not be able to provide you with sales, they can give you brand awareness. Having that interactivity and engaging with your social media followers also increases your chance of coming up in different search engines for individuals who are in your area.

When it comes to creating your social media presence, the most important factor above all else is that you are engaging on Instagram. You should consider posting at least once a day. Remember that Instagram also has the potential for you to utilize the story option, which has shorter videos available for 24 hours, to keep your customers even more engaged.

Facebook has many ways for you to create online communities to have a close following that you can have discussions with, people who can give you feedback or requests for future projects. They might provide you with insight as to things they didn't like and any other issues they had with your product or your company.

The more that you engage on social media, the

more chance you have of people interacting with your product. Engaging your online customers means that you prompt discussions with them. You should be reaching out as frequently as possible to discuss different things about your business. Even if somebody just comments on a picture and says that they love your product, you can respond with an emoji or by saying, "Thank you." The algorithm works in favor of posts that have a lot of interaction on them, so creating that engaging content is absolutely essential. You should respond to as many direct messages as possible. But remember, there are also a lot of spam accounts online as well, so not every single account who messages you is going to be a legitimate one.

Navigating the online world can be quite scary, especially for individuals who didn't grow up with the Internet. There are plenty of brand experts out there who can help. You don't have to hire a full-time employee: there are many contract workers who are willing to get online a couple of hours a week to work on your social media presence, who work with several companies and don't require a full-time wage.

When it comes to what you actually post online, get creative! Of course posting pictures of your products, your animals, or even your employees as they are working can be a great way to give customers a better insight into their products. You can give sneak peeks for products that are coming up, and have exciting surprises. However, think about other creative ways to expand your audience. You can post time-lapse videos of you harvesting a field. You could have tutorial videos on how to plant different seeds. all People consider farms to be relaxing environments. You could set up a live stream of your livestock, as people enjoy watching animals and having that on us background noise. All of this can be done on YouTube, and you can have shorter clips on Instagram to encourage cross-promotion of your social media accounts. The online world is an endless source of potential growth for your brand, so don't underestimate these free tools that are literally at your fingertips.

HOW TO MAXIMIZE PROFIT

$$\mathcal{R}$$

*A*t one point, I had a client who was losing money every other year.

He could go from making six figures one year to losing just as much as he gained the next year. The issue was, he was using the same crops over and over again. He grew nothing but cabbage. He had all the equipment necessary, so he never really saw the point of trying to branch out. I realized the reason his crops were doing so bad every other year is because it wasn't the optimal growing condition for them. Instead, we came up with a plan for him to alternate his crops. We even came up with a plan to purchase some animals to help contribute to the soil.

He switched between soybeans and cabbage every other year, oxidizing the soil in between each cycle. Before he knew it, he was back to making a consistent amount every year, as he was distributing to major retailers. It was a rapid progression, and one that was simply done when he really began to look at where his profit was getting lost, rather than always focusing on how to make more and more and more.

Instead of trying to think about how to focus on playing off your biggest strength in business, notice where your weaknesses are. Sometimes, they can act as a hole in the bottom of your boat, so no matter how much you might gain, you're still losing at a consistent rate.

Maximizing Opportunity

Maximizing opportunity means that you're taking advantage of every last aspect of your business to make sure that you're getting the most from your money. One important thing to remember about maximizing your opportunity is to consider how you can include year-round crops into your production. This means that you never have an offseason, whether it's the summer, winter fall or spring. You always have a crop ready to produce. Of course you can't do this if you are a pumpkin farmer. Those aren't going to be grown all year round and they certainly wouldn't be profitable anytime other than the fall.

In order to really make the most of your land, consider having a greenhouse.

It can be much more expensive than crops, because you have to pay for the electricity to run it, and creating that ecosystem indoors has its own separate biological process that will take special time and consideration to perfect. However, in the long run, it can provide you with a much higher opportunity to continue generating revenue all of the 365 days of the year.

The most important way to maximize your profit opportunities is to diversify. Let this be part of your mission statement one way or another. Try including as many opportunities as you can as they come to you. When I say take on opportunities, I'm not talking about taking on as many projects as possible. An opportunity is when you see the potential for something and you take advantage of that. Anybody could go out and buy 10 different seeds to farm. That's not what I'm talking about. What I'm saying is: if you notice that you have an excess snail habitat going on in your garden, maybe you could eventually farm those snails. If you realize that you have an old empty barn that's not doing anything 365 days of the year, why not turn it into a greenhouse to increase your crop-growth land?

How can you have plants growing at all times to always be productive? Remember downtime is just as important, so don't get too overwhelmed. You still need moments for your land to replenish itself, and for you to have moments of rest.

Think of non-farming related opportunities that you can include on your property. Perhaps you have an old barn and instead of turning it into a green-house, maybe you could transform it into a bed and breakfast. You could have rooms to rent out on Airbnb. Not only might people be looking for a place to stay in your area, but they might also want that homey, farm feeling. You can also have fun activities like self-picking. We often think of this, when it comes to pumpkins.

It's fun to get a group of friends and go out to the pumpkin patch and find your perfect pumpkin for Halloween. You can also do this with many other kinds of produce, like strawberries, apples or toma-toes. It's a way for you to have free labor, while also ensuring that people are getting the most out of their buying experience. They get to choose the juiciest, ripest products, and they'll remember them more as they're at home, making dishes with the things they worked hard to pick. When it comes to having your own pick-farms, remember people aren't always as respectful as they should be, so that can come with its own potential damages.

If you have a lot of extra space, but not necessarily the time to farm on it, why not rent out a few lots for a community garden? You can have people pay rent for the actual land, or maybe you can negotiate a commission out of the sales of what they are producing on your land. This is something for you to work out with the people involved, but consider renting out your space rather than just using it yourself.

As we already discussed, take things online. YouTube offers monetization through targeted ads to individuals who have a certain number of subscribers and views. Typically you'll want at least 200,000 collected views across your videos, and at least 1000 subscribers to maintain monetization. You can create relaxing videos. You could have ASMR by having you plowing a garden on a sunny afternoon. You could have time lapses of crops growing. You could have tutorials on how to farm. You can film tutorials on how to create lovely, rustic flower arrangements, or create recipes with your products. You can simply have vlogs where you give a day in the life of a farmer, and you show people firsthand what it means to be a part of your farm. Get creative with your content, and know that there are endless opportunities online for you to connect with an audience and make passive income in a different way.

Remember aquaculture and your potential to not

only harvest fish, but to create a space in your land where people can come and do their own fishing as well. You can rent out plots of your land for motorhomes, for people staying in your area for vacations. You could also have an animal daycare, or maybe a petting zoo with a fun, immersive experience for the whole family. The opportunities are going to continually present themselves to you, so don't be afraid to reach out and take them as you see it.

Specialty Crops to Grow

One way to maximize your opportunity is to consider specialty crops to grow. This isn't just plants. Also, think about animals and insects that you could farm. For example, worms and snails can be very profitable. People use worms for fishing or even to add into their own soil. Snails are becoming increasingly popular, not just for food, but for different products as well. Honey can be a very profitable product, and people love buying honey straight from the farm.

Mushrooms are also very easily grown and don't take much effort from you, but can be a very specialized market. You should also consider bonsai trees. There are also many landscaping trees that are harder for people to grow on their own, but something that you could provide to them. As we discussed earlier, products like leafy greens, tomatoes, carrots, and other root vegetables can be very easy and very profitable. However, for that same exact reason, others might be making this their market too. In order for you to really hit that niche, you should search for specialty crops that are in demand. It could even be something a little more exotic like dragon fruit, which could be grown in a greenhouse even if you live somewhere cold.

By finding specific market niches, you're solidifying an audience that's likely to come back on a consistent basis, knowing that you are the source for this specialty item.

Byproducts

Great farmers know that nothing ever goes to waste. When you are a farmer, you are more connected to nature than most people. You understand the cycle of life and how growth works. You recognize that everything, no matter how small, is worth something. You've watched a seed smaller than a grain of rice turn into a crop that you were able to propagate.

For these reasons, you can appreciate the value

that is found in every last thing you come in contact with. As far as maximizing your potential and increasing your profit goes, look for byproducts of farming that you can sell.

One of the most popular byproducts for farmers to trade with others is manure. If you have animals, that means you have a lot of manure.

It also means you have healthy soil that you can sell to others. This is necessary for creating the food that we eat. If you think about it too much, it gets a little weird, but a good business person sees the opportunity in what others might assume is just waste.

With all of the crops that you are growing and producing, you likely have a lot of leftover seeds. You can use these seeds to replant even more crops, but you can also sell them to other farmers. You can also package them up and hand them out to customers at local farmers markets, even if you're just doing it for free. These are still great ways to reach out to people and give them something a little extra to make them feel special. They'll have a greater connection to you and be more appreciative that you have acknowledged their contribution to your business.

If you are slaughtering animals on your site, many of the leftover parts that are also seen as useless are actually very useful and in demand, Bones are great for broth and some of the parts you might normally throw away, such as hearts or other organs, can be sold on as food for dogs or cats. Look for ways to cross-feed your own animals. This isn't just from animal products either, but also from the food that you're actually growing. A farm should strive to be as self-sustaining as it possibly can. You should be able to make money from the money that you're investing back into the farm. It should be its own continual financial system, because it's an ecological system. The money that you make can be reinvested back into the company through the maximizing of these different opportunities.

Connecting to Customers

Connecting to customers is your way of creating a long-lasting following that continues to come back to you. When you have happy customers, they go home, and they tell people about why they're happy. They share their products with others, and that spreads the word. Then the individuals just introduced to your products have a chance to become happy customers who then spread the word again. It's a continuous cycle and you want to try to achieve that. Not only do happy customers keep coming back, but they also help provide you with greater insight.

As a business coach, I know that customer service can take a toll on people. Working in customer service can be incredibly taxing. A lot of people complain nonstop and it can be frustrating to try to accommodate every little demand. I've had a number of clients who were concerned with maintaining a high level of customer satisfaction, but it seemed like nothing could keep all customers happy, and their employees would also make things difficult.

An employee isn't always going to be as concerned with creating a repeat customer as you might be. The most important thing you can do is remember that each customer is an individual. Sometimes when you get hung up in making huge profits, it's hard to not see a customer as just a way to have a profitable transaction. Although it's not right, it's something that happens to the best of us, especially when our biggest concern is growing our company.

However, by looking at people as transactions, it makes it more frustrating to start really listening to them and hear out their concerns. I've had a lot of clients who also felt like they were already knowledgeable in a certain subject. They didn't think they needed any help from anybody else and they would grow frustrated whenever people would offer advice. Take all the feedback from your customers and use it when feasible. Of course, you're going to hear some ridiculous requests. A customer might tell you that you should start growing a completely new crop that's impossible to grow during that season. They might tell you that you should build a barn, or do something else that's wildly expensive. Even when they offer potentially annoying, or seemingly unachievable bits of advice, thank them.

Appreciate that they care about your business and are trying to offer ways to connect to you. Quite often, people can simply be lonely and be seeking some fulfillment in our capitalist society. We've really robbed customers of the chance of connecting to their brands. We go to the store, we buy what we need, we check out and we leave. The purchasing process is strenuous and empty. It doesn't have to be that way. People should be excited about the products they're getting from you. They should want to go home and make a delicious meal. They should feel connected and fulfilled with the things that you are providing to them. This relationship is one that will become long-lasting and help ensure that these people keep coming back.

When people do offer up concerns or other comments on something that has left them less than satisfied with your product, again, accommodate them. Give them refunds, or provide them with a discount next time they come back. You don't want to give everything away for free all the time to people just because they complain. But at the end of the day, it's important to keep people happy and satisfied. They can go to the store and get vegetables and check out and go home. They're choosing you because it's an experience. To be able to give back directly to your community through supporting small businesses is very fulfilling. It's a rewarding opportunity for them, and they are specifically seeking you out in order to do this. By acting as though they're simply transactions, or by providing meaningless interactions, you are robbing your customers of the special experience they're seeking out from you rather than these big box stores that you're in competition with. Remember that personality trumps everything else. Don't be afraid to get to know people, ask their name, ask what they do. Don't ask them what their political affiliation is or if they go to any churches, but find personal touches in conversations that don't dive into these topics.

Memberships and Exclusive Perks

One way that you can connect to individuals and establish a more meaningful relationship with repeat customers is by offering exclusive perks, or even memberships.

Some small farms have memberships where they allow patrons to come in and pick out their products. They might have a box and you get to fill that box for $30 every month. They might have a pick time, and arrange when they get to come in and pick their own flowers and make their own arrangements.

You should seek to provide these exclusive perks whenever you see those opportunities. Not only are you creating a stronger need for these customers to return, but you're also increasing profits in unique ways. It will be easier for them to have that connection and want to be more committed to you. Not only are you providing them with a product, but you're also giving them a special experience when you offer up memberships.

Exclusive perks can come for repeat customers as well. You could give them simple reward cards, where you punch a hole in a piece of paper every time they come back and when they buy 10, they get one free. That's pretty much the most basic way that you can foster loyalty. You could also offer discounts to specific groups online. You might give 10% off to all of your Instagram followers if they prove that to you when they are checking out.

These exclusive perks make your customers feel special. Therefore, they'll seek out those good emotions through your brand, helping your business thrive by spending more money with you.

Reinvesting

Growing your profits and maximizing the potential of your business is all about reinvesting.

To start, you make $10,000 your first year from farming. That's great. However, that's not sustainable for life, so you need to look for ways to upgrade. First and foremost, this can start with looking at space. How can you increase your space to grow even more?

I always encourage my clients to begin with a

quarter of the land that they have. I'll recommend even less for beginners, or for extremely massive amounts of land. By starting with a quarter, that means for the next four to eight years, you have potential growth opportunities. Of course, you could speed up the process and start by farming the entire plot of land within your third year. However, by increasing progressively each year, you're giving yourself a chance to gradually fit into new roles.

It could be daunting to think about farming on that land when you first start off but remember how much more talented you will be even after your first year.

Once you have expanded to all corners of your own land, then you'll want to consider purchasing more land around you to increase your potential even further. Remember to think indoors as well. Do you have a basement or an empty barn that can also be used for growing your business?

Other upgrades include increasing or improving your equipment. Can you go from something home-made or small to something that provides faster production? For example, if you are working on a small quarter portion of your lot, you might be hand-harvesting everything. Can you invest in better equipment to streamline these processes?

Whenever you reinvest, you're also giving your-self a major tax break. Any reinvesting you do is going to count as an expense, so even though you might have made a certain amount of money in the first quarter, you can use that to invest in the second quarter, meaning that your total income will be less.

Make sure to take care of necessary repairs and upgrades, such as simply painting a barn, repairing or even rebuilding it.

Building a farm isn't a get rich quick scheme. It's all about gradually growing over time and creating something incredible. Your farm is going to be passed down from generation to generation. It's going to be something that sustains the environment and the community, and gives something back to Mother Earth.

Don't rush this process and remember it's a slow and steady climb to the top.

SEVEN COMMON MISTAKES MOST FARMERS MAKE AND HOW TO FIX THEM

❧

*O*ut of all of the mistakes that I see people make, having the wrong mindset can be the most damaging. In this chapter, I'm going to touch on a few common mistakes I want you to avoid, and issues that many farmers can run into. Keep in mind as we go through these, a huge part that plays a role in these mistakes is having the wrong mindset.

Farming can seem so simple on paper sometimes.

You put something in the ground, you water it and let the sun shine down on it, and eventually you have something you can sell. In reality, it takes a lot of mental effort. You have to be self-motivated, you have to get up early in the morning and work all day, and you have to be honest with yourself and confront issues as they arise. You have to be a business owner and a farmer all at the same time, and that can take its toll.

When I really look back at all the clients that I have helped in the past, even outside of just farming, it is always the mentality that can hold you back. This includes thinking that you know too much, or not being comfortable with asking for help.

It could also be about not having the passion and motivation to really reflect on your business practices in a healthy way. Even if you can't succeed based on the things I've laid out throughout this book, at least make a promise to yourself that you will not make these mistakes.

Starting too Big

I have worked with clients who started off with $3,000, and I have worked with clients who started off with $300,000.

Regardless of the initial investment that somebody made, the most important thing to remember for either situation is to not overdo it.

I've worked with many individuals who were overly ambitious. They had grand ideas and hopes and dreams for their company. That is absolutely wonderful, and I would never discourage that in somebody. However, sometimes people do get overly excited about this process and forget practicality. They put every last penny they have towards the wrong investment. When it comes to farming, people can get overly ambitious and they end up taking on too many projects at once. The people that start with thousands and thousands of dollars have the money to buy a lot of livestock right away. However, things can happen so quickly, and it's never good to jump into the deep end of the pool if you don't know how to swim. Even when you do know how to swim, if you're not aware of the waters you're diving into, there are other mistakes that you can make.

Starting too big means biting off way more than you can chew and taking on projects that are only going to keep you held back in the end.

The best word of advice that I can give you to avoid the mistakes of anybody that I've discussed so far in this book is to start small. Pick one thing at a time. If you want to start growing spinach, then start growing spinach. If you want to start growing every kind of leafy green that's in a salad, do this after a month or two of starting. If you can't even get a seed to germinate and turn green, then you can't invest all of your time and money into this process. If you are here, you likely have some background knowledge on farming already. You should also probably know then that going in too deep too quickly can mean risking too much. Farming can be really fragile sometimes. Whether you have a finicky plant or sick animals, things can get messy so much quicker than they can get successful. For that reason, don't put all your eggs in one basket and instead focus on really getting to know yourself as a business owner. It's only once you're immersed in some of these situations that you truly recognize your full potential.

Too Many Projects

We just talked about starting too big. Now you might be thinking, "Isn't starting too many projects the same thing?"

Yes and no.

The second biggest mistake that I see clients do is overexerting themselves on too many projects. It's not that they're unsuccessful and it's not that they don't have the money, but it's that they're not giving their 100%.

I had this client who had a wonderful green thumb. She could look at a seed and it would turn into a flourishing tree overnight.

Of course, not literally, but she was so good at taking care of her farm and plants that I wished every client was as talented as her. She had great products, but unfortunately, she was overexerting herself: at one point, she was trying to grow 24 different vegetables at the same time.

The thing was, there were so many missed

opportunities along the way, and many small minor setbacks that kept holding her back. For example, she might harvest one vegetable and then move on to the next, only to forget about it and have it sit out in the sun wilting away the entire day.

There were times when she would overlook produce and realize only once she had gotten to the farmers market that some of it was moldy, or that it had bugs crawling on it.

The thing was, she was very talented and good at what she was doing, but she wasn't good at doing so much. She was giving 20% of herself to everything. Instead, I told her to cut it down by 75%. I made her get rid of her 18 worst selling products. Instead, she stuck it out with just the top 6 within the first year. Her business was already doing so much better because she had refined her efforts. She was using her considerable talents to make sure that each one of these products was perfect, rather than making sure that 24 different projects were just okay. Once she finally got that routine down to a science, then she slowly started adding other products back in. This would be one thing at a time. So she might go from nine vegetables to 12 vegetables over a year.

At this point, she's capped out at 16 and I think that's the best for her at the moment. She has no desire to hire extra employees, so if she does want to continue to grow in the future, that's totally fine. But I remind her consistently that she needs to limit herself to not ignore important aspects of her work. She's managed to create something so much more substantial because she's narrowed it down to the things that she does the absolute best. Everything else was just filler to make her feel more productive, but in reality, it was taking time away from her, time that could have been spent putting more effort into what was necessary.

Being Impatient

One frustrating thing many of my clients do that makes me want to grab them and shake them is that they are so impatient! Hm, I suppose that's a little impatient of myself as well.

Some businesses are week to week with how owners can see results. If you have a bustling restaurant, that means one weekend you could make more money than the rest of the month. If you have a clothing store, we all know that the right weekend means that the items can fly off the shelves until those are empty. Unfortunately, farming takes a lot longer than that. If I have a client who is looking for a market to get into, I make sure to gauge their patience. How quickly do they want results?

Farming is one area where you are not going to get those quick results. You have to be a very patient individual. The thing is, once that does come it floods you. Once you harvest and start selling it provides you with so much more than you would have thought. Not only is it fulfilling because you'll see your shelves empty, so to speak, but because you know that you grew those products. You put the time, the work and the effort in, and even for that reason alone, it's such a fulfilling endeavour. If this does not appeal to you, then I urge you to truly consider if farming is something that you're comfortable with.

The thing about farming is that you also cannot rush it. You could spray chemicals to make your products grow faster, you can use grow lights so that your plants flourish all year round, but it's still going to take time. There is no fix or solution to make farming an instant thing. Unfortunately, there are going to be problems that set you back as well. You might have a certain portion of your crops die off, which means you have to replant them. You could have sick animals, or maybe a litter is a lot smaller than you thought it was going to be during breeding. We also have to remember that farming is not something that happens all year round. There will be on and off seasons where you aren't making as much money as you did before. As we discussed in the last chapter, you should look for ways to maximize your opportunities so that you can make money all year round. But not everybody is able to do this with the resources that they have. While you should still try to have those cover crops in between, these aren't necessarily profitable. You're still working at times when you're prepping for the next seeding or harvest, but you're not making any money, and that can be very upsetting for people. While you might make $5,000 in one month, the next month you might make $1,000 because it's just not the right harvest. If numbers like this scare you, or if you feel you are too impatient, then again, reconsider if farming is the right business for you to pursue.

Ignoring Branding

The world of farming as a very diverse one.

I have met farmers who are completely spiritual, liberal, free-flowing, and connected to nature. They have passion about the earth and they feel a deeper meaning in what they're doing. But I also have met farmers who know nothing else. They grew up in this environment. They're rather conservative and a little more closed off. They're serious, straightforward, and they just want to get their work done every day. Both types of clients require my help when their businesses aren't doing very well.

One thing that I noticed in a good percentage of my clients is that they ignore branding. You could have the greatest product, but if it looks bad, no one will buy it. Alternatively, your product could be the absolute worst, but if it looks like gold, then people are still giving you their money. One thing I have to remind both types of clients is that branding is important if they ever hope to get out of the rut they are in.

Sometimes my more spiritual, free-flowing

clients don't care about branding. They think it's part of a capitalist ideology and they reject the very thought of putting a logo or marketing concept on their crops. Then I have the very stern face of traditional farmer clients who don't really know what a logo is and don't really care. They have no desire to get on social media and use hashtags or come up with an aesthetic for their company.

I get it, marketing is not everybody's passion, and figuring out your brand is hard.

However, it's a huge part of making sure that your business flourishes and grows. If you don't feel comfortable doing the things that we discussed, such as creating a YouTube channel or having a logo, there are experts out there willing to do this. It might cost you more, and there is definitely an initial investment in having a brand expert or social media manager come into your business to help. However, it can also increase profits in ways that you didn't think were possible.

Sometimes I have clients who ask me, "How can I do better? How can I sell more? Why is my company doing so badly? I have products, my plants are growing. But nobody's buying them."

I remind them it's not about changing the pH of your soil or trying to get a different flavor in your crops. It's not about raising your animals differently. Sometimes it's simply how you show the product that makes the difference of who decides to purchase it. Clean your produce off. Make sure it looks aesthetically pleasing at the farmers market. Make it easily accessible and have people want to pick it right up off the shelf and take it home. It shouldn't be piles of dirty potatoes they have to dig through or unsightly carrots with the roots still hanging out everywhere. These products should be carefully taken care of to make them the most pleasing possible.

Not Asking for Help

Another thing about some farmers is that they are afraid to ask for help. They think it makes them look weak. There's a huge, traditional portion of the farming community in which people are very concerned with maintaining their masculinity, and appearing as though they don't need any outside resources.

Then there are individuals who believe they're scientific experts and they know every last bit about farming, so they don't want to ask for help. They might approach it in a more modern way and reject any sort of advice from their predecessors. However, help can be one of the most powerful tools you have. Whether you're simply asking for advice from somebody who's been there first, or you have to hire a staff of three people, asking for help is not a sign of weakness. Taking care of yourself is important, but not everybody is able to do that.

I want you to think of a quick analogy. This is

one thing that I use to remind my customers who are too afraid to reach out for that external help. I asked them: why is asking for help scary?

Sometimes they answer that it makes them look weak or vulnerable. Other times they simply shrug their shoulders and don't know.

Now I want you to consider a situation. Imagine that you're walking down the street and you see that there's a little child trapped under a car. How they got under the car, I don't know, but the fact of the matter is, they're trapped there, and they need your help. What makes you look stronger?

In situation one, you try to pick up the car yourself. You do everything you can, but you're simply not strong enough to lift it, meaning that the child does not get the help they need.

In situation two, you use all the resources necessary to ask for help. You call for help and you look around you, quickly screaming for assistance. You manage to find four to five people who come and help you lift up the car together. While you might have thought you were strong enough to do it on your own, you weren't.

Which situation do you believe makes you look stronger? The obvious answer is asking for help. While it can be scary and make you feel vulnerable, it can be the exact way to grow your brand.

Ignoring Problems

A huge mistake I never want you to make is to

ignore issues or ignore any aspect of knowledge necessary to troubleshoot or diagnose issues as they come to your farm. Many clients play ignorant and they don't do the necessary research to figure out what their issues are. Don't leave the state of your crops or your livestock up to fate.

Are your plants looking yellow? Are they brown and crispy? Do your animals seem sick? Are your pigs acting funny? Are your chickens especially noisy?

One small minor crack in the glass can lead to the entire window shattering.

While some of these little things seem like no big deal, do not brush them off. Never stop doing research. While farming can seem pretty cut and dry and easy to understand in certain ways, it's also a science. It's a process that requires you to consistently check in with new knowledge. You should always be seeking out as much information as possible, especially in this specific niche in which you are involved.

By playing ignorant and ignoring potential issues around you, you could be setting yourself up for future failure. I actually had one client look me in the eyes and tell me as a 42-year-old man, he hadn't read a book since high school. He almost said that he was proud. I looked at him straight back and I said, "How can you manage to run a business if you haven't read a book since then?"

Farming might not seem like the most academic process, but in order for it to be successful, it should be. Never stop seeking out knowledge. Never just hope that things will just get better. Never assume that something is natural. Even if you realize that the fungus growing on your plants is actually helping them, you still have to learn about why or how in the first place. People will let their ignorance take over and then wonder why things didn't work out in their favor. Don't let yourself become one of these types of individuals, and instead focus on growing your knowledge as you grow your profits.

Overlooking the Business Side

One of the biggest and most common mistakes you can make is pretending as though this isn't actually a business.

People get into farming because they like it. Nobody who doesn't absolutely loves farming has ever come to me needing help to get started in this business. This is usually a passion project for people. It's something that they used to do when they were little, that they also did since then, or that they've simply always had an interest in. Because of that, it can easily become a hobby. The moment that you stop treating your farm as a business is the moment that you make room for error for your profits. In order to stick to a business plan, you have to treat everything as normal operations. This includes making sure that you clock in and out every single day. I've seen too many people overwork themselves because they are constantly working. If you live in the same place where you go to do your job every day. It's hard to clock off. It's easy to always want to keep going. There is always work to do when you own a business, especially when that business is in your own backyard. There will always be more seeds to plant, there will always be more crops to harvest. There will always be new projects to keep up with. There will always be certain things that you have to do to maintain your business, but that does not mean that you should never stop working. You can quickly become burnt out if you do so.

Another thing you have to remember is to not keep it casual. One of the biggest mistakes that I noticed in the beginning, is when my clients begin to give their products away for free. Their neighbor thinks now they can just grab a handful of produce since the farmer has so much of it. Their friends and family will all come over and grab the best of the bunch. They'll give some for free to friends and not be considerate of how each item of produce is a potential profit. It's easy to give things away when you're in high spirits right at the beginning as things are taking off and motivation is sky-high. However, this also sets the stage for the rest of the time that you operate your business. You're letting people know that they can keep coming back for those handouts, and the more you let it happen, the harder it is to tell them no after a while.

Of course, giving things away in some capacity can be beneficial. If you're loading up 12 ears of corn for somebody, throw in a 13th or 14th. Of course, you can make up a nice little basket for your neighbor, or family and friends to help spread the love. However, remember it is not an all you can grab buffet. When it comes to growing your produce at the end of the day, this is a business and you need to treat it as such in every aspect possible.

ACCOUNTING AND TAX REMINDERS
FOR FARMERS

∞

One of the easiest cases I had as a business coach was with one overly ambitious farmer who was very, very confused about his finances.

He decided to take all of the business tax and accounting into his own hands instead of having a third party do that for him.

He wasn't very well versed in tax law, but he did want to save money and figured it was easy enough to do on his own. However, he was hardly making any money despite all the hard work that he was putting in. He couldn't seem to turn a profit.

When I first started talking to him, I was a little confused myself. It seems like he was taking all the right steps for marketing and doing everything possible to be smart about the costs. I then asked to take a look at his taxes from the past few years. When I laid eyes on his accounts, my immediate response was to freak out, but instead all I could do was chuckle.

I asked him if he knew what an expense was. He looked at me confused.

It turns out this entire time, he was only writing down his profit, but never any costs of the business.

He worked completely on his own and didn't have any employees. It was a smaller farm with produce you would take to local farmers markets. He didn't have huge equipment that costs thousands, but he had plenty of expenses that added up.

Once I explained to him that he could write off costs, he got excited. He thought farming was a complete out-of-pocket experience and didn't realize he'd be able to save so much money on his yearly income tax.

Needless to say, this meeting only took a few hours to help him understand all that he could begin to write off.

As you're reading this now you probably think, how could anybody not know what expenses are, and that was my exact thought too. But unfortunately, a lot of people are not well versed in taxes. It isn't a subject that's greatly taught in schools, and the forms can be deliberately confusing at times. He was missing out on hundreds of income, every year, and hundreds from tax breaks every year as well, because he was not properly monitoring his income. We fixed his problem pretty fast and now his business is thriving. I want everybody reading this to recognize the importance of knowing their financial stuff. Anytime that you are unaware of something, you have to consult an expert; while you might seem like it's fine to just take a guess or a gamble, don't let yourself do this. Even missing out on $10 can make a difference in some situations.

Accounting for Your Farm

When keeping track of your own business, don't forget the strenuous process of having to check in with your records on a consistent basis. It's important that you are keeping track of every little thing, no matter how big or small. This is one of the most annoying and tedious parts of the job for my clients. In the beginning of our time together, I make sure to really instill that they have to be very diligent with every expense and cost that they track.

The main reason for this is for their own protection. If they, and you, are to ever get audited, it can be a total headache. You will be tracked for every purchase and expense and the more proof you have the better.

By tracking these expenses, you can also collect data that can be used to determine where your money is going and whether or not that is contributing to, or taking away from, your success as a company.

To better track your expenses, it's important to have a laptop or tablet where you're doing a lot of your business. This way you don't have the excuse of, "Well, I'll enter that when I get home to my desktop." That never works. Farmers don't like to sit behind office desks that much, so after a long day of working outside, the least exciting thing is going to be to sit behind a desk and enter numbers.

Keep all your information with you digitally so it can autosave online through various programs, like iCloud. This way, no matter what happens to your actual devices, you will always have access to your information. Don't trust the old school notebook or notepad: you can drop them into a bucket of water or a puddle, and lose all your sums and numbers.

Make sure that you have a separate bank card for all of your business purchases. It's not always recommended to take out loans or credit, but if you are taking out a credit card anyway for other reasons, having a business one offers its own perks. Sometimes you can get rewards for traveling or other business expenses, depending on your credit program.

You should save your receipts, but by having separate accounts, it's much easier to be able to go in and see exactly where you've been spending your money.

Don't be afraid to shell out for some expensive tracking software either. Again, it's a big upfront cost, but it can save you so many headaches, especially if you're not a tech or tax-savvy person.

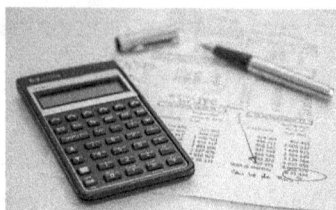

Track your time as well because this can come in handy for employment purposes. Not only will you be able to have this information ready when potentially being audited, but when you have to hire help you'll know exactly what is needed. You can look at your tracked time and see you've worked 65 hours in a week, meaning you should hire someone on to help out with at least 20 a week to cut down on your time and boost productivity.

Writing things down should be a daily activity. You should allow at least five or ten minutes to this just as you would any other basic operation on the farm. Then, give yourself at least one day every few weeks to balance your books. Are you spending money in the right places? Are you on track with your financial goals? What is worrying you and what requires more attention? By keeping up with your records in this way, it becomes much easier to keep track of everything you need to do for optimal profits.

Having backup paper records is helpful, but keep these organized from the moment you get them. Keep things separated in a file cabinet instead of letting them pile up on your desk. Have a system organized before starting rather than letting it be an, "I'll get to that eventually," kind of task.

It's incredibly helpful to also ensure you automate all of your bills online. You can have them be taken directly out of your business account, so they are easy to track. If you pay a month in advance for many utilities, some companies will also let you pick the date. For example, if all of your utilities hit the 5th of the month, but you have a credit card payment coming in on the 26th, you could potentially have it swapped to the 5th to have all your bills taken out at once. Missed payments not only rack up extra fees, but it could make your business look bad and have negative effects on your credit score.

There is more to accounting for your business that you will discover as you dive deeper into your own company, but let's look at a few more things to understand when breaking down the accounting process.

Understanding Income

When starting any business, many people come to me concerned. "What is my income? Do I get a paycheck? Do I write a check to myself?"

There are some LLCs or corporations that will give the owners a paycheck, but that won't be the case here.

If you do want to eventually become an LLC, you would be on the payroll only if determined by you and the rest of those in charge of the company, but you would also receive income from the total profits of the business. You can choose to reinvest that back into the company, but this is still going towards you and your income.

For most of you reading, you're likely going to be the sole proprietor which means that everything your business makes is everything that you make. If your company made $20,000 last year, you would count that as your total income.

The thing to remember here is that your gross income is going to be far less as you will be taking expenses out. As far as tracking income goes, that is rather simple as long as you are keeping up with the accounting. At the end of the day, determine how much you made from sales. If you made $10, you would mark that down. If you made $1,000, that would also be noted. It doesn't matter how big or small, it's still money that you made. At the end of the week, you can add this up and keep track of your weekly sales.

Expenses are harder to track because sometimes you might forget that something was an expense. This is why having a separate company card is helpful. It can be annoying sometimes. You might go to the grocery store and buy food for your family only to remember you need something like paper towels or cleaning supplies for your farm. Having that separate transaction might seem tedious, but it still makes it easier for you to track these purchases later on, so keep a record of every last thing you buy for your company and remember to separate it from simple personal expenses you have for yourself.

Recording Expenses

An expense is anything that costs money that is required for your business operations. A $10,000 tractor is an expense. A $1 pen is an expense. Big or small, if you spent a penny or more on something and you are using it in the production of your business, it counts.

As a business coach, I am all about making sure you track every single one of your expenses. This is how you ensure you are maximizing your profit and avoiding unnecessary tax charges.

On a basic level for your farm, expenses will be things like

- Animal feed
- Water
- Electric
- Heating/gas
- Equipment
- Tools

- Soil

You also have to consider things for your home office, such as:

- Computers
- Desks
- Chairs
- Pens
- Supplies

Expenses aren't just physical things they also include

- Employee salaries
- Repairs
- The use of your home as an office

Whenever you are spending money on your company, it is essential that you write this all down. Just as you track your income consistently, you must also keep a note of your expenses to balance everything at the end of the day. Are you on track with your goals? Are you keeping in line with your projections for costs?

The more you track, the easier it will be to see your weaknesses. Maybe you're spending way too much on feed. Could your electric bill be lowered? All of these things add up quickly, so even though it might seem silly to track pens, it could make a difference. If you spend $50 on pens every year for a decade that's still $500 you can write off. If you do this with pens, paper clips, cleaning supplies, and all that other small stuff that you might not normally care about, this can rapidly add up, saving you thousands over the years.

Important Insurance

We touched on insurance at the beginning of the book, but I want to take a final look to serve as a reminder of the importance of various insurances to protect your company. Accidents happen and you don't think about them until too late. No one assumes a tree is going to fall on their truck and smash their windshield. You don't imagine that a bear is going to come into your farm and attack your goats. You don't predict that a random gas leak is going to cause a huge barn fire.

These events can be devastating. No one wants to think about them, but unfortunately, as a business owner, you're only setting yourself up for failure if you don't.

Insurance can't always be lumped, but if you find this opportunity, it can be helpful. There are so many types of insurance spread across many areas that it can be challenging to find a company that covers them all!

Farms are dangerous, so remember to cover yourself in all areas of liability. This includes any type of injury to you or someone else, and any damage to the property.

Employee insurance is important for worker's compensation. Liability insurance and worker's compensation insurance are two different things, so remember that both are necessary when hiring employees or having fences and "keep out," signs posted around your property.

Having different types of damage insurance is also important. This might include hurricane, tornado, flood, and earthquake insurance. It's crazy to think about, especially knowing you could very well never live through a tornado in your life. However, if you don't have insurance and a tornado destroys everything, it's crazy to think about NOT having it.

You have to have insurance on every vehicle you have, even if it never leaves your property.

I had a client once who had an old beat-up truck he drove across his property to move supplies. It wasn't registered, so he never bothered to pay for insurance. It was in the family and only served as a means to help carry things across the property.

Well, one day he was driving around and looked away momentarily. He was constantly driving around on his property with no issue, so he wasn't overly cautious.

He ended up hitting one of his own pigs. Unfortunately, the pig had to be put down due to the injuries, and it was a tragic scenario.

What exacerbated it was the fact that this loss of livestock was not covered by insurance! He had all of his animals under his policy, but that didn't matter as it was hit by a vehicle. There was a loophole in his insurance, and the automobile owner's insurance was responsible for any damages to livestock should an automobile accident occur.

I use this story to always remind clients to read the fine print of their insurance policies. At the same time, remember it's also important that you have insurance for the right things! No one thinks they're going to hit their own pig on their own farm, but accidents happen. That pig managed to get out of the fenced area that day, and it ended in tragedy and a financial headache.

Tracking your expenses and everything else you've put into your company is also important because it provides you with necessary insight into what you spent money on, should you need to make an insurance claim.

For example, let's say that you spent $300 on a new TV for your home office. Your home burned down and now you're out a TV, among many other things. You claim this TV on your insurance policy and are only given $150 for it because that was the lowest listed price for a TV of your size in terms of market value. You paid more for the specific brand and features, but that doesn't always matter. This is why you need to be specific so you can ensure you get a fairer price for these products. You likely wouldn't get the entire $300, but at least $200 or $250 is better when it comes to replacing damaged goods.

Taxes for Farmers

Once tax season arrives for many, it's a joyous time. All of that interest-free loan money you gave the government now gets to come back to you!

Unfortunately, farmers know that tax season isn't always the best, as now it's time to pay large sums of taxes.

First and foremost, as a sole proprietor, remember to file your quarterly taxes. These are done four times throughout the year to make sure that you don't have to pay a huge amount right in the middle of tax season.

Remember to set this money aside as part of your budget when considering income.

Don't fret if you can't pay your taxes all at once. For example, if you made $15,000 last you, you could owe over $500 but you might also be struggling and not able to come up with that right as your taxes are due. As long as you stay in contact and up to date, they will work with you on payments. You will only be in serious trouble if you don't pay for a very long time and ignore any of the IRS's attempts to reach out. You would still likely just be fined and your wages would potentially be garnered before you would ever be arrested. Convictions that are more serious occur because people are lying about their income and hiding massive funds in a deliberate attempt to avoid paying taxes on earned and hidden income. Some of my clients get rather fearful when they think about not being able to pay their taxes and wonder if that means they have to leave their family for a cell. Don't fret! No one can force you to go to prison for not paying, so long as you are honest about the situation the entire time.

As you do your taxes, you will balance between your income and your expenses. It's a lot simpler than what people fear, but remember all the available tools out there, both online and in person, to help you with this process.

There are many tax breaks for farmers as well, so be sure to check out your state laws to see what they can do to help give you a little boost. Property tax breaks are common for farmers, as many areas want to encourage farming. Remember to consider what it means to be qualified as a farmer in your state as well. Most will state that any earned income over $1,000 counts as a farm, but not every place is so lenient. In some areas you might have to even earn over $2,500 for 2 consecutive years or more, so keep updated with what the regulations are for your area.

AFTERWORD

Farming is fun. Farming is scary. Farming is unpredictable. Farming is fulfilling.

Farming is whatever you make of it.

If there is one thing I hope you take away from this book, it is that you can do this, as long as you are smart about it.

Of course, we all think we are smart. Most ignorant people have no idea that they're ignorant!

Approach everything with awareness. Think of the worst possible scenarios, but don't let that keep you from reaching for things you know are attainable. This can be a hobby, but it can also be a solid foundation for a lifelong business.

Where should you go from here?

First, you should check in with your business plan and adhere to what you believe is the next step. Do you have a name? A logo? A mission statement?

Remember to start with those, and let them carry you on throughout the rest of the process.

Never be afraid to reach out and take advantage of the resources that are out there for your continued success. Farming can come so naturally to humans, so don't be afraid to go out there and get what's waiting for you.

REFERENCES

Caldwell, D. (n.d.). Tax Write Offs for Farmers. Retrieved from https://smallbusiness.chron.com/tax-write-offs-farmers-12399.html

Ebeling, A. (2012). Farm Like A Billionaire -- Harvest Tax Breaks. Retrieved from https://www.forbes.com/sites/ashleaebeling/2012/06/06/farm-like-a-billionaire-harvest-tax-breaks/#1c39d40c5777

EPA. (n.d.). Laws and Regulations that Apply to Your Agricultural Operation by Farm Activity. Retrieved from https://www.epa.gov/agriculture/laws-and-regulations-apply-your-agricultural-operation-farm-activity

Live Oak Bank. (n.d.). The Importance of Reinvestment Through Retrofitting. Retrieved from https://www.liveoakbank.com/agriculture-resources/reinvestment-through-retrofitting/

NOLO. (n.d.) 50-State Guide to Establishing a Sole Proprietorship. Retrieved from https://www.nolo.com/legal-encyclopedia/50-state-guide-establishing-sole-proprietorship.html

PennState Extension. (2019). Agricultural Business Insurance. Retrieved from https://extension.psu.edu/agricultural-business-insurance

Turbotax. (2019). How to File Federal Income Taxes for Small Businesses. Retrieved https://turbotax.intuit.com/tax-tips/small-business-taxes/how-to-file-federal-income-taxes-for-small-businesses/L8ghn14sF

Wickison, M. (2020). 27 Ways to Make Money From Your Small Farm. Retrieved from https://toughnickel.com/self-employment/small-farms

www.ingramcontent.com/pod-product-compliance
Lightning Source LLC
Chambersburg PA
CBHW031534040426
42445CB00010B/536

From the ER

to the

Stars

A True Story by Edward Meek

With additional Perspectives from

Char Meek (Mother)

Dave Meek (Father)

Wendy DeYoung (Sister)

Christine Meek (Wife)

Cover Artwork by

Taran Meek (Son)

From the ER to the Stars

ISBN: 0692344667
ISBN-13: 978-0692344668